CAP WIGINGTON

Clarence W. Wigington in the 1940s

Minnesota Historical Society

CAP WIGINGTON

An Architectural Legacy in Ice and Stone

David Vassar Taylor

WITH Paul Clifford Larson

MINNESOTA HISTORICAL SOCIETY PRESS

Published with the generous support of The Saint Paul Foundation and the
Katherine B. Anderson Fund of The Saint Paul Foundation.

www.mnhs.org/mhspress

Designed by Dennis Anderson
Map on page 105 by CartoGraphics Incorporated
Manufactured in Canada

10 9 8 7 6 5 4 3 2 1

The paper used in this publication meets the minimum requirements of the
American National Standard for Information Sciences—Permanence for Printed
Library materials, ANSI Z39.48-1984

International Standard Book Number
0-087351-415-7

A Cataloging-in-Publication record for this book is available from
the Library of Congress.

CAP WIGINGTON

FOREWORD

IN 1972 I TRAVELED to the Schomburg Center for Research in Black
Culture, part of the New York Public Library, and began research for
an article on African American architects. I was assisted by Mr. Ernest
Kaiser, a research librarian, who had painstakingly assembled handwrit-
ten note cards on a variety of subjects over many years. Mr. Kaiser's file
noted a "Clarence Wesley Wigington (1883–)" as "City Architect" with a
further reference to an article in the Urban League's *Opportunity Magazine.*
The article described Wigington as "Chief Designer and Senior Architectural Draftsman in the Department of Parks, Playgrounds and Public
Buildings of the City of St. Paul, Minnesota." It included a photograph of a
bespectacled man who looked both modest and reserved—characteristics
not usually associated with architects.

I was puzzled, however, by Mr. Kaiser's descriptive term "City Architect" and the article's reference to "Senior Architectural Draftsman." As
an architectural student, I knew the difference between an architect and a
draftsman. Furthermore, the article stated that Wigington had the good
fortune to have worked under city architects who appreciated his exceptional abilities. My repeated calls to various Minnesota agencies yielded
no reference to a city architect by the name of Wigington. Mr. Kaiser's
notes listed several other illustrated articles on black architects, but none
of them mentioned Wigington. Finding no images of buildings or other
sources to document his position or work, I filed Clarence Wesley
Wigington away for future reference—as others had probably done since
his retirement in 1949.

In stark contrast to the card on Wigington was another referencing one of his contemporaries, Paul R. Williams (1894–1980), who was featured in the March 1928 issue of *Opportunity Magazine* with three illustrations of his designs for YMCA buildings in Los Angeles and Hollywood. First mentioned in a 1917 issue of *Crisis Magazine* (a journal of the NAACP), Williams, ten years Wigington's junior, had been gaining fame and exposure on the West Coast. He became one of the country's preeminent black architects, known for designing the private residences of many Hollywood film stars.

Wigington was one of only fifty-nine black architects, artists, and draftsmen who were listed in the federal census of 1910, as his career was beginning; far fewer than half of them are known. Nearly half of the practicing African American architects of Wigington's era were educated or employed at the Tuskegee Institute in Alabama. Tuskegee, established by Booker T. Washington in 1881, was built by its students, in an effort that demonstrated Washington's self-help concepts and vision. Washington recruited Robert R. Taylor (1869–1942) to teach and head the school's Department of Mechanical Industries. Taylor, the son of a North Carolina builder, entered MIT in 1889 (the year that Wigington's first employer, Thomas R. Kimball, graduated); he is considered the country's first African American graduate of a major architecture program.[1]

Taylor became Washington's trusted architect and chief campus designer after his graduation in 1892. Under Taylor's skillful direction, many of the country's pioneer African American architects matriculated at Tuskegee, including Wallace A. Rayfield (1874–1941), John Anderson Lankford (1874–1946), William S. Pittman (1875–1958), and William A. Hazel (1850–1929). As Wigington began his apprenticeship with Kimball in 1902, Lankford was opening one of the early African American architectural offices in Washington, D.C. Pittman, who completed his Tuskegee studies in 1897 (a year after Lankford), earned a second architectural degree in 1900 from Drexel Institute, then joined Lankford's Washington practice briefly before opening his office in 1905.

Black churches and schools were the major clients of these pioneer African American architects. At the 1908 Annual Conference of the African Methodist Episcopal Church, Lankford was appointed "Supervising Architect" of the A.M.E. church. Lankford's responsibilities included the directive that "all plans, specifications, supervision and drawing of any and all kinds and character, be furnished by him as far as practicable."[2] Indeed, Lankford and Wigington may have met as Wigington completed his plans for Omaha's St. John's A.M.E. Church.

There were other African American architects of the time who, like Wigington, found their way into the profession without attending Tuskegee. Julian F. Abele (1881–1950) completed architectural studies at the University of Pennsylvania in 1901. Among his major designs were Harvard's Widener Library, the Duke University campus, and several Gilded Age homes in Newport, R.I. Paul R. Williams, the Hollywood architect, graduated from Los Angeles Polytechnic High School in 1912. He, too, began as an architectural apprentice and acquired some formal training, but earned no degree in architecture. It is interesting to note that Williams and Wigington were friends. In the early 1950s, the two were responsible for re-establishing the Los Angeles chapter of the National Technical Association (NTA), the professional organization of black architects, designers, engineers, and draftsmen.

Williams and Wigington now have yet another thing in common. They are the subjects of the only biographical works to explore the professional profile of African American architects. In 1993 Karen E. Hudson published *Paul R. Williams, Architect: A Legacy of Style,* a biography of her grandfather. This book on Clarence Wigington, written by David Vassar Taylor with the assistance of Paul Clifford Larson, is a pioneering treatment of Wigington's education, training, professional practice, and personal life. Don Wong's exceptional photographs vividly document Wigington's evolution and maturity in style. The nearly sixty buildings attributed to Wigington in St. Paul make up one of the most extensive collections of works by an African American architect, exceeded only by Williams. And as important as the architectural study is Taylor's success in placing Wigington within the socio-cultural context of his time. Both Williams and Wigington epitomized W. E. B. Du Bois's notion of the Talented Tenth. Wigington was a leader, and where possible he used his considerable influence to advance opportunities for black people.

The photograph of Wigington gracing the cover of this book, taken by prize-winning African American photographer Gordon Parks, provides an interesting contrast to that first modest image of Wigington I saw in 1972. Parks captures Wigington in front of the Highland Park Water Tower, cigar and hat in hand, showing his strength, perseverance, and confidence. He is the creator, the architect, and he is firmly in charge. This is the Cap Wigington whose works we enjoy today, and the man whose legacy enriches the life of a community.

Richard Dozier, Arch.D.
Professor of Architecture
Florida A&M University

PREFACE

A S A Y O U N G professional in the 1980s, I served as director of the Minority/Special Services Program at Macalester College in St. Paul. Among the highlights of that association was the "Great Lives" program, which invited people whose lives had helped transform American culture to spend a week on campus in dialogue with students about dedicated lives of service. None of the guests had started life by seeking fame. Recognition came to them because they led principled lives in service to humanity. These were ordinary citizens who accomplished extraordinary things.

On one occasion I hosted Dr. Benjamin Mays, the legendary educator, scholar, and former president of Morehouse College. He was then in his late eighties, and his unassuming manner and quiet dignity served to underscore the impact of his work as architect of a new race consciousness in America. His leadership paved the way, much like the biblical John the Baptist, for better things to come. As I reflect on the extended conversations I had with Dr. Mays, I remain impressed by how, from such humble beginnings, great things can be accomplished.

My research on the life of Clarence Wigington has filled me with the same awe. During a period of great social change in American history, he labored, as both a professional and a private citizen, to build bridges across the divide that separated races. He was a practical man, conservative at his core, but principled. The buildings he designed were built to serve. The leadership he provided in St. Paul's African American community was an extension of his belief in returning the benefits of blessings bestowed on him.

Although I did not know Clarence Wigington, our lives intertwine. I was born about the time that his career in the St. Paul City Architect's Office was ending. His work as president of the board of the St. Paul Urban League, under the leadership of then–executive director S. W. Owens, made it possible for blacks to obtain meaningful employment; through those efforts, my mother found work as a nurse's aide at Miller Hospital. Wigington and his family attended St. Philip's Episcopal Church, my church home for fifty years. I attended John Marshall, a school building he designed. I remember his beautiful old home on the corner of St. Anthony Avenue and Grotto Street across from the elementary school I attended. One of my favorite places as a child was the Como Park Zoo, which he probably had a hand in designing. And for a brief period, while attending graduate school at the University of Nebraska, I lived in Omaha, where I remember attending worship services at St. John's AME Church, an early Wigington building.

My master's thesis on John Quincy Adams, the veteran editor of *The Appeal,* a St. Paul black newspaper, was my first exposure to Clarence Wigington in his historical context. Editor Adams was one of Wigington's mentors; he died just as Wigington was settling into his career with the city. My Ph.D. dissertation, "Pilgrim's Progress: Black St. Paul and the Making of an Urban Ghetto 1870–1930," explored the development of St. Paul's black community, attempting to capture the spirit of those pioneers who laid its foundation. In each of these works, Wigington's contributions were overshadowed by the legendary leaders of his time.

This book gives Clarence Wigington his due. It is about both the legacy of the man and his contribution to the architectural heritage of St. Paul. Adams's death in 1922 signaled a transition in leadership to a younger generation of activists and educated professionals. Wigington was then approaching forty; the next twenty years would be the most productive of his architectural career. These were also the years of his greatest impact on the character of St. Paul's black community.

Today, more than half a century after leaving his position as architectural designer for the city of St. Paul, Wigington and his work continue to have a profound effect on many lives. Coming of age in an era that marginalized African Americans, Wigington and his contemporaries attest to certain strength of character that allowed them to succeed. Principled men and women with a strong work ethic, they succeeded in part because they seldom strayed from their beliefs. The municipal buildings that Wigington designed, an extension of his beliefs and values, are still used by thousands of people daily.

This book would not have been possible without the assistance and support of surviving members of Clarence Wigington's immediate family: his daughters, Mildred Bohanon and Muriel Pemberton; grandchildren Michael Bohanon and Caroline and Gayle Pemberton; and numerous great-grandchildren, all of whom share a strong sense of family pride. Wigington himself left few glimpses into the private man behind the public persona. But granddaughter Gayle Pemberton provides a poignant insight into his world of family, friends, and social life in her memoir, *Hottest Water in Chicago: Notes of a Native Daughter,* in which she recalls grandparents "Papa" and "Nana" Wigington and reflects on Clarence's lifetime accomplishments.

Architectural historian and author Paul Clifford Larson wrote chapters two and four of this book and the appendix listing Wigington's buildings. Larson's extensive knowledge of early St. Paul city government, insights into the workings of the City Architect's Office, familiarity with the architectural character of the city, and candid assessment of Wigington's architectural legacy were invaluable. His niece, Ursula Larson, now pursuing a master's degree in architecture, was a principal researcher on the project. Bob Olsen provided details about the ice palaces.

Last but not least, I'm grateful for the undying support and dedication of the Friends of Cap Wigington Legacy Committee of The Saint Paul Foundation. Under the leadership of Jean Hart, committee members Clint Hewitt, Bob Olsen, Marilyn Porter, and Judith Van Dyne labored for four years to make Clarence Wigington a household name. In addition to spawning a quarterly newsletter, numerous magazine and newspaper articles, public programs, and private tributes, their diligence resulted in the renaming of the Harriet Island Pavilion in Wigington's honor. A special thanks to Paul Verret, The Saint Paul Foundation, and the Foundation's Katherine B. Anderson Fund for unwavering enthusiasm and financial support for this project.

CAP WIGINGTON

Wigington in about 1905

Carolyn Pemberton

1

TO BE YOUNG, GIFTED,
AND BLACK

SOMETIME IN November or December of 1914, Clarence Wigington, his wife, Viola, and their two young children boarded a train in Omaha, Nebraska, bound for St. Paul, Minnesota. A handsome man, impeccably dressed, with a light complexion and a formal manner, Wigington was a fledgling architect of some note in his hometown. He came from a respected family, had an excellent work record, and enjoyed influential contacts in the white professional world. These assets notwithstanding, he was a "colored" architect in a city where the racial climate resembled that of any southern town of the era. With a family to support, thirty-one-year-old Wigington needed steady employment. St. Paul, he hoped, would have the right combination of variables to enable him to earn a living in his chosen profession.

Wigington's move to St. Paul coincided with the "Great Migration" of African Americans in the early years of the twentieth century. In search of better employment opportunities and housing, they came by the thousands from the rural South to industrial cities in the North. The trickle that began in the years preceding World War I soon became a flood. Between 1915 and 1920 approximately one million blacks left the South, some spurred by promises of jobs in war-related industries, others simply fleeing from stifling racial oppression. Cities to the east experienced the greatest influx of southern blacks. Detroit's black population, for example, grew by 611 percent between 1910 and 1920. During that same period, the black population in Minneapolis grew by only 51 percent and St. Paul registered a modest increase of just 7.4 percent. By war's end, however, 49.1 percent of Minnesota's black population had come from the South.[1]

Unlike many other migrants who sent for their loved ones after securing employment, Wigington brought his family with him. They took up temporary lodging in St. Paul with his older bother Frank, a janitor, at 355 Arundel Street. Clarence also arrived with resources—enough money to rent a small office in the Court Block Building. From there he planned to launch the next phase of his career.[2]

It was not, however, the best time to relocate a private architectural practice. With the flames of war engulfing Europe, the economic climate was uncertain. A panic on Wall Street had slowed plans for municipal building in St. Paul; construction of private residences had suffered as well. So it was fortuitous that in May of 1915 Wigington's wife saw in the newspaper a civil service job posting for architectural draftsmen. She encouraged him to sit for the examination. It was a time when few African Americans had found their way into the field of architecture. But Wigington felt ready to make his mark. He awaited only the right opportunity—and it was not long in coming.[3]

CLARENCE WESLEY WIGINGTON was born April 21, 1883, in Lawrence, Kansas, the fourth boy of twelve children. His parents—Wesley Wigington, a Texan of mixed racial heritage, and Jennie Mary Roberts, a Missouri schoolteacher—moved the family to Omaha when Clarence was five months old. There Wesley worked a succession of jobs as hod carrier, janitor, factory worker, and laborer.[4]

Perhaps following Wesley's work, the family moved seven times between 1884 and 1908. The first two neighborhoods in which they lived were located in a mixed working-class area of Omaha. The next was a black neighborhood on the North Side, then an almost all-white neighborhood at the edge of the North Side, followed by another mixed neighborhood. The family's last two residences were in Walnut Hill, a predominantly white neighborhood of imposing houses. It may have been the Wigingtons' biracial background that enabled them to move freely between racially mixed and racially separated neighborhoods. Or it may have been that racial segregation in housing as it would be practiced later had not yet solidified in Omaha. Whatever the case, young Clarence learned to move comfortably between the two worlds, a quality that would come to serve him well in his professional life.[5]

Wigington family residence in Omaha's Walnut Hill neighborhood

Paul Clifford Larson, 1999

The family's peripatetic ways also may have delayed Clarence's formal education. He did not begin school until the age of 10, then transferred from one to another and back again as the family moved. Despite those disruptions, he finished eight years of elementary school studies in just five years, entering Omaha High School in 1898. The next year he gained public recognition for his budding artistic talents when, at age fifteen, he won three first-place certificates at the 1899 Trans-Mississippi World's Fair in Omaha for best drawings in pencil, charcoal, and pen-and-ink. Impressed by his exceptional artistry, two of his elementary school teachers, a Miss Johnson and Miss Emily Dorn, urged him to enroll in art school, offering to pay half his tuition. So from 1900 to 1904 young Wigington studied art as a night-school student, first at the Studio-Atelier of Professor Alfred Juergens, then at the studio of Professor J. Laurie Wallace. There he received instruction in drawing, oil and watercolor painting, design, and clay modeling.[6]

After completing high school in 1902, Wigington was encouraged by a family friend to consider the field of dentistry. But he needed a job and, through the intervention of another family friend—Mrs. Marie Brown, private secretary to nationally renowned architect Thomas R. Kimball—he secured a position as clerk in Kimball's architectural practice. Personally tutored by Kimball and his associates, chief draftsman George Prins, and structural engineers Frank Brazee and Loren Rustad, Wigington was soon promoted to student draftsman, then to junior draftsman. In 1908, after completing assigned construction specifications for the All Saints Parish House, he left his position with Kimball's firm and opened his own office in Omaha's Barker Block.[7]

That year there were important developments in his personal life as well. On July 8, after a brief courtship, Clarence married Viola Lessie Williams, whom he had met at a dance. Born in Oklahoma and raised in Atchison, Kansas, twenty-year-old Viola was described on their marriage license as "colored"; in fact, she was very fair—a mixture of white, Cherokee Indian, and black ancestry.[8]

During the first year of his practice and his marriage, Wigington busied himself with several major projects. It is unclear whether they came

Wigington designed this Omaha house, his first private commission, for black custodian Isaac Bailey in 1908.

Paul Clifford Larson, 1999

to him as private commissions while he was still in Kimball's employ or whether he landed the projects after establishing his own office. One project, a home for Mr. and Mrs. Isaac Bailey, garnered Wigington significant public notice. Designed and built in 1908, the Bailey residence was called by the *Enterprise*, Omaha's black newspaper, "the first that was ever built in Omaha from the plans of a colored architect and it is the opinion of every person that has seen it that his efforts have been very successful." Another project was the initiation of plans to remodel St. John's A.M.E. Church, the first black church established in Nebraska, where Wigington's mother was a member.[9]

In 1908 Wigington was awarded his first commercial commission, the design of a small potato chip factory in Omaha. Shortly thereafter he entered a national comptition sponsored by *Good Housekeeping* magazine and won first prize for the best two-family brick dwelling. But four years would elapse before the duplex design would be constructed, and in the meantime jobs were slow in coming. Encouraged by a brother-in-law who ran a dry-cleaning business in Sheridan, Wigington closed his Omaha office in 1909 and moved to Wyoming.

In Sheridan he set up his practice hoping to capitalize on his factory commission. Instead, he found himself vying for a share of a small market with several other local architects. To gain a foothold, he entered a competition for the design of the new county courthouse and jail. Although he was a strong contender, after five weeks of deliberations the contract was awarded to a competitor. Needing to support himself and his wife, he took a job as manager of the factory he had designed. Unfortunately, the business venture was short-lived.[10]

Not long after this episode, Wigington read an announcement in the Sheridan newspaper about a building program at the National Religious Training School in Durham, North Carolina. He immediately wrote to the president, Dr. James Shepard, for permission to participate in the bidding process. He won the competition for plans to construct an administration building and men's and women's dormitories. With an advance for that work, he and Viola returned to Omaha in 1910.[11]

His sojourn in Sheridan had lasted little more than one year. It was the nadir of his career. Back in Omaha, both his professional and his family life flowered. Viola gave birth to their first daughter, Muriel Elizabeth, in 1911, followed by Sarah Mildred in 1912. Meanwhile, Clarence opened an office in the Karbach Block that he shared with a black dentist. By 1912 he again had an office of his own, this time in a building at 220 South Farnham Street rented to Wigington, the dentist, and two black lawyers.

Wigington served a mixed clientele, designing homes for black physician Leonard E. Britt in 1912 (above) and white business executive Hollis M. Johnson in 1914. (right)

Above photo by Paul Clifford Larson, 1999; right photo Omaha City Planning Department, 1982

The next year he advertised a full range of services in the *Omaha City Directory*: "Complete Blue Prints and Specifications for all Classes of Buildings, Bungalows and Residences a Specialty."[12]

Between 1912 and 1914, Wigington served a mixed clientele of blacks and whites, designing at least eight residential projects: an apartment

Broomfield and Crutchfield Apartments, built in 1913

Omaha City Planning Department, 1982

Zion Baptist
Church, rebuilt in
1913 after a tornado
destroyed much of
North Omaha

Paul Clifford Larson, 1999

Cornerstone, Zion
Baptist Church

Paul Clifford Larson, 1999

building; three duplexes, among them a pair built to the *Good Housekeeping* plan and known as the Broomfield and Crutchfield Apartments; and four houses, including a bungalow for Dr. Leonard E. Britt, a leading organizer of the Omaha chapter of the National Association for the Advancement of Colored People (NAACP). After a 1913 tornado devastated North Omaha, Wigington was chosen to design a new 1,200-seat structure for Zion Baptist Church, the largest black congregation in the state, at a cost of $100,000. Despite these successes, his future in Omaha apparently did not seem promising to him, perhaps for reasons similar to his experience in Wyoming. He decided to look elsewhere for opportunities.[13]

2

AMONG EQUALS

A T T H E D A W N of the twentieth century, St. Paul was a city filled with promise. While the country still groped for its economic footing after the Panic of 1893, organizers of the Paris Exposition of 1899 declared St. Paul the most livable city of its size in the nation. As the capital of Minnesota and the head of Mississippi River traffic, its place at the vortex of the state's cultural and economic development was assured. Even after a sprawling, coast-to-coast rail network began shifting the flow of people and goods from water to land, the city remained strongly positioned between the established commercial centers of the East and the fledgling cities and vast timberlands and farmlands of the West.[1]

St. Paul, ca. 1910: Robert Street, looking south from East Seventh Street

Minnesota Historical Society

There was, however, trouble in paradise. The rapid growth of industry and commerce had left much of St. Paul's infrastructure behind, at the same time that city government and city services were expanding exponentially to serve the burgeoning population. By 1910 that expansion began to teeter on its 1880s foundations. Schooling took place in crowded, outmoded buildings, and the growing profusion of automobiles jolted over roads designed for horse and wagon. Fire stations were themselves major firetraps, and police stations were little more than carriage houses with a desk. Public use of green space so far outstripped city planning that parks and playgrounds created as a refuge from the urban jungle threatened to become its defining component. Over all of these growing pains hovered an ineffectual bureaucracy laden with political intrigue and clouded by conflicting lines of authority and responsibility.

Into that scene stepped Clarence Wigington in 1914. What he saw around him when he got off the train in his newly adopted city were a decaying railroad station and the ragged edges of a once-glorious warehouse district. Yet this was not a place of meager buildings or a diffident population. Downtown hummed with new construction. And an informed citizenry was poised to demand that its tax dollars produce public achievements in line with the prosperity of the private sector.

One of the catalysts for change was a nationwide vision—what had come to be called the City Beautiful. Its signature was an ordered array of monumental, classically inspired civic buildings, usually arranged on a grand downtown esplanade, with parkways radiating outward to the residential streets and green spaces of the city's neighborhoods. Three short years after Wigington arrived, a Union Station with a proper temple front would replace the Queen Anne patchwork of the old depot. Third Street would begin widening into Kellogg Boulevard, spawning a new generation of office buildings and warehouses. And a grand library would rise on Rice Park.

As if to prove that the seam between old and new in the city's fabric could not be sewn by local talent, the design of these enhancements was awarded to out-of-state firms. But even while the projects were underway,

Transformation of Third Street into Kellogg Boulevard, looking west from Robert Street, 1933.
The City Beautiful movement ushered in a new era of civic building in St. Paul.

A. F. Raymond photo for the St. Paul Dispatch, Minnesota Historical Society

the city moved to marshal its own architectural forces into an office run by the city itself. Union Station and the public library would inspire a far-reaching new order in St. Paul civic building, one put in place over the next generation by local architects operating under the aegis of city government.

Politics had as much to do with the coming mandate as aesthetics, for St. Paul was in the process of radically reordering the way it did business. After years of cronyism, financial waste, and muddled lines of responsibility, citizens had voted in 1912 to install a commission form of government. This innovation would be the second great catalyst for a new generation of civic buildings. Under its rewritten charter, the city was run by a mayor and six elected commissioners, each with clearly defined authority and responsibilities. The remaining city employees—school administrators and teachers excepted—were hired under a Civil Service Bureau. This form of government and the bureau that brought people into it soon opened the door to architect Wigington.

Government under a commission was a Texas invention, originating in Galveston in 1901. Its watchwords were solvency and efficiency, two increasingly scarce commodities in the cloud of corruption that hung over many American political institutions at the turn of the century. As the new kind of civic management spread northward into Kansas and Iowa, it took on a populist agenda. By 1914 commission government charters commonly authorized nonpartisan ballots, citizen initiatives, and a merit system for hiring and promotion. These innovations were put into place primarily to increase the responsiveness of government to the needs of its citizenry. But they were also a boon to those who wished to serve in the government itself. Civil service examinations opened participation in government to persons of merit without reference to political connection, social status, gender, or race.[2]

In St. Paul the new charter went into effect June 1, 1914. The commission under which Wigington would serve was Parks, Playgrounds, and Public Buildings, already in place as a department under the previous government. What was new was the Office of City Architect. Before 1914 city building projects, including public schools, had been awarded to architects at large

Charles A. Hausler,
St. Paul's first City
Architect

*Minnesota Historical
Society*

on the basis of proven work, prior city connection, or some form of competition. Under the new charter, design and construction oversight of all buildings paid for with city money had to come from the city itself, through its architect and his office staff.

Exempted from civil service classification, the City Architect was an administrative appointee. Rather than seeking a well-known architect of proven ability, Louis Nash, the first commissioner of Parks, Playgrounds, and Public Buildings, chose a neophyte with first-rate business and political skills, good connections in the architectural community, and a high level of personal ambition. Twenty-five-year-old Charles A. Hausler began service as City Architect on June 13, 1914. A native of St. Paul and graduate of Mechanic Arts High School, Hausler had apprenticed with an impressive succession of architects: Clarence Johnston in St. Paul, Harry W. Jones in Minneapolis, and Solon Beman and Louis Sullivan in Chicago. In the two years before his appointment by the city, Hausler obtained his architectural license and began cultivating close professional relationships in St. Paul's growing fraternity of progressive, young architects.

When work in his city office stalled for want of funding or authorization—as it often did—Hausler juggled his official responsibilities with a flurry of independent commissions under four successive partnerships. During his early years of service, Hausler also drew on the talents of those partners for an assortment of city projects. Whether that constituted an end run around the Civil Service Bureau or merely filled the gap between the startup of his office and the hiring of a drafting crew is difficult to establish. In any case, Hausler quickly proved himself a master at getting things done in a frequently chaotic political milieu.[3]

Often more caught up in controversy than in architectural activity, Hausler himself was at the center of the storm. Six weeks after his appointment, he grew impatient waiting for the Civil Service Bureau to act and appointed another young man, George Wirth, as his first draftsman. Though a novice himself, Wirth even sat on the examining board for a time, until the men he helped to hire replaced him. More serious issues arose when Hausler attempted to carry out New York architect Electus Litchfield's specifications for the new public library, designed before Hausler had taken office. His youth and slim professional credentials made him an easy target for the machinations of local contractors and Litchfield's own firm. But the mayor and Commissioner Nash backed Hausler up, and the authority of the City Architect's Office was established.[4]

The first civil service exam for architectural draftsmen was finally held October 21, 1914, not long before Wigington arrived in the city. Eight men stood for the exam; three passed and two were appointed. The appointees immediately went to work on plans for branch libraries at St. Anthony Park, Riverside, and Arlington Hills, built with a Carnegie grant to the city. If there was any doubt that the City Architect's Office could produce first-class architecture, the construction of these splendid library buildings from the designs of Hausler and his staff must have dispelled them.[5]

Amid growing pressure from the public and the commissioner of education, Hausler's office then turned its attention to the city's parks and overcrowded schools. Another exam for architectural draftsmen was held on May 25, 1915. This was the exam that brought Clarence Wigington, at his wife's urging, into city service. Eight men stood for the senior architectural draftsman's exam; eight others took an exam for junior architectural draftsmen held at the same time. Wigington proudly announced to his friends that he had passed with a score of 84.78, the highest in his group.[6]

Wigington thus became the country's first African American municipal architect. His hiring occurred at a time when few African Americans were practicing architecture in any capacity. It was all the more remarkable because Wigington lacked one of the formal qualifications for senior draftsmen—an academic architectural education. The fact that the University of Minnesota's Department of Architecture was established only

CLARENCE W. WIGINGTON
Architectural Draughtsman, St. Paul.

The civil service commission h proven to be quite a good thing the colored people of St. Paul w can "make good" and several are n holding good paying positions in t city departments. One of the m notable cases is that of Mr. Claren W. Wigington, the subject of th sketch, who now holds the position architectural draughtsman.

Mr. Wigington took the city ci service examination for architectur draughtsman on May 25, 1915, a passed, making a rating of 84.78, th being the highest record made by a of the eight applicants taking the e

CLARENCE W. WIGINGTON.

amination at that time. He receiv a temporary appointment June 25 and was permanently appointed Se 2nd in the office of the city archite of the Department of Public Buildin just because he was ready and "ma good."

Mr. Wigington came to St. Pa about a year ago from Omaha, Ne where he followed his profession himself for five years. He also spe five years in the office of Thomas Kimball, architect, Omaha.

He designed three large buildin for the National Religious Train School at Dunham, N. C., and made the designs for many church lodge buildings and residences in rious parts of the country.

Mr. Wigington is happily marri has three interesting children, and sides at 582 Rondo street.

the year before may have allowed a temporary suspension of the education criterion. It is also possible that Wigington's portfolio of his Omaha work and a recommendation from Thomas Kimball were impressive enough to substitute for an architectural degree. In any event, experience was given a weight of 20 percent in the exam, with another 20 assigned to mathematics, 10 to a written report, and the remaining 50 to expertise in architecture itself, measured by the applicant's facility in making technical drawings, writing specifications, and drawing sketch plans.[7]

Even after he posted the highest score, Wigington's job apparently was not assured. A better-known local draftsman, Raymond Eisenmenger, entered the City Architect's Office before him. Wigington and several others had to accept temporary appointments until funds or authorization from the city came through. The temporary term of appointment officially began June 25, 1915; Wigington's full appointment commenced August 23. His beginning salary of $110 a month was five dollars more than the minimum for senior draftsmen. For a decade Eisenmenger and Wigington would compete for the lion's share of school building designs, until Wigington finally emerged on top in the mid-1920s.[8]

At the time of Wigington's employment, Hausler's office was still grappling with the city's new way of doing things. For all the vaunted efficiency of the commission form of government, one of its elements— a mandate that all building construction be managed in-house—created years of administrative and financial turmoil. An issue of special concern to the City Architect's Office was a directive from the commissioner of Parks, Playgrounds, and Public Buildings that city building projects be run under force account rather than contract. This meant that general contractors would bid on the job, but the city would hire labor, buy all the materials, and supervise construction. Though designed to save money, the force account method led to lengthy postponements in construction starts, frequent work stoppages, and cost overruns for which there was no provision in the annual city budget.[9]

Despite widely acknowledged needs across the city, school construction in 1915 reached no further than a few remodeling projects and the

Wigington joined the City Architect's office just in time to have a hand
in the design of Como Park Elementary School, built 1916.

Don Wong, 2000

initiation of plans for Ames School and a pair of one-story elementary schools in the Randolph Heights and Como Park neighborhoods. The design for Randolph Heights School, published the month before Wigington stood for the civil service exam, was of particular importance. The Bureau of Education intended it to serve as a model for all new elementary schools in the city.[10]

Assigning Wigington a clear role in any of these projects is problematic because the design process for each was well underway before his employment in the City Architect's Office. In fact, attributing designs of individual buildings to any particular draftsman on the City Architect's staff is risky business at best, for the City Architect himself had ultimate responsibility for all design work emanating from his office. The problem of attribution during Hausler's tenure is compounded by the absence of any documentary means for determining who might even have assisted in the creation of construction documents. Only Hausler's name appeared in local press notices on new city buildings, and the working drawings provided no place for draftsmen's initials.

Como Park Elementary School was a rare exception. Wigington scrawled his name on the working drawing of the main elevation and in later years claimed credit for the school as a whole. His claim of authorship is bolstered by the fact that drawings of the school's principal façade were published during the period of his temporary appointment. The temple front of the school's central bay certainly has many affinities with the portico of Wigington's Zion Baptist Church in Omaha, a neoclassical set piece from which he would continue to borrow for more than a decade. The school's floor plan, however, owes its main features to the Randolph Heights model.[11]

Hausler's ambitions notwithstanding, the first seven years of the City Architect's Office were marked by a constant struggle to get projects off the drawing board and into St. Paul's neighborhoods. Small projects took years to accomplish and an undisclosed number of municipal projects were shelved, the probable result of financial uncertainties occasioned by World War I.

With disappointingly little to do in his city post, Wigington moved late in 1916 to Davenport, Iowa, to work for the Gordon–Van Tyne Company. One of the largest house-building corporations in the world, Gordon–Van Tyne hired a revolving cadre of skilled designers and architectural illustrators, publishing their plans in a series of catalogues advertising homes that could be ordered "ready-cut" and assembled on site. Wigington must not have found designing for mass production to his liking, for the following spring found him back in St. Paul. A letter of recommendation cited him for "turning out some of the best and finest-looking drawings that have ever been done in this office." Unfortunately, it is impossible to single out his work in surviving Gordon–Van Tyne catalogues; the firm followed common practice in the mail-order house business by omitting draftsmen's signatures from their published drawings.[12]

Wigington did not go back to the City Architect's Office immediately, choosing instead to work for local home building and financing company T. D. McAnulty during the construction season of 1917. Several substantial McAnulty homes went up on Summit Avenue and in the Macalester-Groveland neighborhood during the next few years. Wigington, however, was assigned the task of designing nine smaller houses, quite possibly all in the same development.[13]

Wigington's year of wandering ended in the winter of 1917–18, when he returned to the City Architect's Office. Hausler immediately set him to work on what would become Wigington's first complete contribution to the city's architectural heritage. In March 1918, John Quincy Adams, editor of *The Appeal*, visited Wigington in his office, interviewed Hausler, and observed Wigington working on the plans for Homecroft School in Highland Park. The City Architect praised Wigington for being a "very faithful, energetic and capable assistant," for knowing his business thoroughly, and, in the byword of the day, for his "excellent efficiency."[14]

The plans for Homecroft School occupied Wigington intermittently for the next two years, as construction awaited the end of the war. Homecroft was as much a watershed for St. Paul school buildings as it was for Wigington's career. Its design was based on a four-classroom module,

Homecroft's modular plan, developed by Wigington between 1918 and 1920, became the standard for St. Paul school design.

Don Wong, 2000

Entry façade, Homecroft School

Don Wong, 2000

with a façade embracing eight classrooms and back-directed wings that could be extended four classrooms at a time. The rear walls of the main block and the wings were engineered to allow easy removal for expansion. For the next thirty years, the four-classroom module would be the standard for the city's school building program.

Homecroft and its architectural companion, Groveland Park School, were the largest building projects undertaken by the City Architect's Office until the heyday of St. Paul school building in the mid-1920s. More typical of the 1917–22 period were a series of fire station remodelings (mostly for fireproofing) and nine one-room portable school buildings. By 1920 St. Paul had forty-six portable school classrooms, three of them on the future site of Homecroft. Thus much of the energy and talent in the City Architect's Office continued to be dissipated on stopgap projects while Hausler awaited the arrival of funding for more substantial new construction.

One significant advance was made at the close of the war. Phalen Park, in city hands since 1894, finally began to sprout with buildings. A nationwide conversion of scenic parkland to recreational use had begun just before World War I, and St. Paul belatedly joined the movement. A massive bathhouse went up along the west shore of Lake Phalen, and a golf course and clubhouse were constructed on the nearby hills. Park buildings would ultimately become Wigington's forte; the design of these first major park structures at Phalen, however, occurred in 1917 during his absence from the City Architect's Office.[15]

Soon after his return to city employment, Wigington was joined by another young African American, William M. Godette. Eight years younger than Wigington, Godette (known as "Godie" to his friends and soon called "Uncle Teed" by Wigington's children) entered the City Architect's Office as a junior draftsman in 1919. The two were to be colleagues for the next thirty years and close friends until Wigington's death. They were the only two draftsmen in the office to survive the tenure of four City Architects through three decades of service.[16]

Wigington's second stint in the City Architect's Office was an ideal

To augment his
St. Paul work,
Wigington took
outside commis-
sions. In 1921 he
designed this
Northfield creamery
for the Twin City
Milk Producers
Association.

*Norton & Peel photo,
1930, Minnesota
Historical Society*

time for him to put out feelers for independent work, as city construction projects continued to be slowed by the war effort and the triple-digit
inflation that followed in its wake. Hausler, who took outside commissions himself, might even have encouraged it. In 1918 Wigington advertised three modern bungalows, designed to order, on lots near his house
on Rondo Avenue. He had no takers. Two years later he won the contract
for a pair of brick creamery buildings for the Twin City Milk Producers
Association. Built in Elk River and Northfield for a combined cost of
more than $100,00, they were regarded by the association as its most
modern and best-planned plants.[17]

Though busying himself with outside work, Wigington did not long escape the winds of city politics. In mid-1922, Hausler's long-standing and very vocal insistence on one-story design for elementary schools finally cost him his job. Economic considerations swayed the commissioner of education to favor multistory designs for all schools, and Hausler's recalcitrance offended the mayor. Wigington's fate must somehow have been tied to Hausler's downfall; he took a voluntary job reduction to building inspector on July 10, 1922, and resigned altogether on August 15. By that time he had served in the City Architect's Office longer than any other draftsman.[18]

Wigington's express reason for resigning was to take up private practice under the name "The Complete Service Co., architects and engineers." This was more than an effort to give his resignation a positive spin, for he had in hand contracts for $200,000 of work. Published designs for St. James A.M.E. Church on St. Paul's Central Avenue show a near clone of Zion Baptist Church in Omaha. The Pyramid Building, planned by a black corporation called the Pyramid Realty and Investment Company, was to rise at Highland and Lyndale avenues, "the heart of the Negro center" in north Minneapolis; its ground floor was designed to house six businesses, its upper level a thousand-seat auditorium. A third project was a lodge for an African American fraternal organization on Rondo in St. Paul. None of these projects came to fruition, however—at least not to Wigington's plans—and he returned to the City Architect's Office for the third and final time at the end of the year.[19]

On November 24, 1922, Wigington was reinstated as senior architectural draftsman with a salary of $200, near the top of the office pay scale. The new City Architect, Frank X. Tewes, placed Eisenmenger in charge of a spate of school designs over the next year and a half, but in 1924 Wigington emerged as the dominant design force in the office. A year later he became lead architect for John Marshall Senior High School and Woodrow Wilson Junior High School, soon to be followed by Washington High School and Monroe Junior High.

These schools marked a new departure for educational buildings in Minnesota. All had a theater-type auditorium, a gymnasium, and a cafeteria, each with its own outside entrance. Since these large peripheral spaces could be locked off from the rest of the building, they functioned essentially as community centers when school was not in session. As architect of this new generation of schools, Wigington had a unique opportunity to develop plans with both greater flexibility and a bit more architectural dress than conventional school design. All four of the schools remain landmarks in their neighborhoods, though they no longer provide time-shared educational and community spaces.

While Wigington was making his ascent in the City Architect's Office, Godette also took a turn as project architect—for Douglas Relief School in 1924. These were the halcyon years of public building in the city. Not even the great burst of activity under the Works Progress Administration in the 1930s would match the mid-1920s for the volume, variety, and quality of work emerging from the City Architect's Office. The corps of draftsmen circulating through the office were among the most promising of the city's young architects: Carl H. Buetow, Arthur S. Devor, Herman

Wigington was "architect in charge" for many St. Paul schools, including
Washington High School (built 1926), now a junior high.

Don Wong, 2000

Outside entrance to
the Monroe Junior
High School
auditorium, built
1939

Don Wong, 2000

A. Miller, Torell J. Minuti, J. Arthur Salisbury, Eugene V. Schaefer, and Herman H. Witte, to name only those with the greatest longevity. Many of them gave up positions in leading architectural firms to work for the city, and the best were on their way to establishing distinguished careers in their own practices.

As St. Paul's school construction needs began to be filled, the City Architect's Office turned its attention to buildings for two new parks: Battle Creek in the southeast corner of the city and Highland to the west. Battle Creek Park was initially planned as a scenic reserve overlooking the Mississippi River, and in 1924 Wigington designed a log shelter perfectly in tune with the rusticity of its surroundings. Highland Park was quite another matter. Intended from the beginning to serve a multiplicity of recreational needs for a neighborhood expanding to the west, the park lay at one end of a two-mile boulevard running all the way to the new Ford Plant on the Mississippi River. Wigington's greatest contribution to the park would be a monumental water tower at the head of the boulevard.

One of St. Paul's most revered architects, Allen H. Stem, drew up a preliminary design proposal when the city announced its intent to build a tower. But Tewes kept the design in-house and chief responsibility fell to Wigington. Erected on the second highest elevation in the city, Highland Park Water Tower cost $70,000, a princely sum for its day. Though it was originally attributed to the City Architect himself, Wigington received full credit and with it national recognition when the water tower was designated a national landmark by the American Water Works Association in 1981 and placed on the National Register of Historic Places in 1986.[20]

An exquisite pavilion, shared by the golf course and the community, went up in Highland Park in 1929. When Wigington's name first came to public prominence in the 1980s, many immediately attributed its design to him, though the presentation rendering is unsigned and none of the working drawings carry the initials of a project architect. The design also has an openness and ornamental exuberance far from the mainstream of Wigington's work. A safer inference from the absence of initialing would be that City Architect Tewes himself took charge, as he may have done

Highland Park Water Tower, built in 1928, was placed on the National Register of Historic Places in 1986.

Don Wong, 2000

Fire Station #5,
Ashland Avenue,
built 1930

Don Wong, 2000

for a similar community building at Newell Park. Wigington, however, reentered the picture at the close of the 1920s with a number of new fire stations and a clubhouse design for Keller Golf Course.[21]

At the beginning of the Great Depression, when there was yet little sense of how long or severe it might be, work already budgeted continued to swell the ranks of the Bureau of Parks, Playgrounds, and Public Buildings. By 1930 there were 37 employees, the lion's share of them experienced architectural draftsmen. This figure would not be exceeded for the duration of the bureau's activity. Two of the projects underway, the Public Safety Building and an annex to the City Auditorium, were the largest architectural projects ever to emanate from city offices. Wigington played a significant role in both designs. No architect in charge was listed for the Public Safety Building, an austere $400,000 structure still standing on Tenth and Minnesota streets. But Wigington's initials appear on the drawings of column and door details, and the main façade as a whole bears a striking similarity to the simplified temple fronts of which he had been so fond in the 1910s. On the $1.5 million auditorium annex, Wigington has, with some authority, been credited with the design of the façades, Godette with the layout of the seating, and a third African American, Dwight Reed, with the structural engineering, making it, in the language of a contemporary report, "almost a Negro project." Years later the auditorium would be named after NAACP leader and St. Paul native Roy Wilkins.[22]

By the time Charles A. Bassford stepped in as City Architect in 1930, Wigington was the acknowledged but untitled head of the drafting room.

Roy Wilkins
Auditorium, built
1929–30

Don Wong, 2000

For the next fifteen years he would be architect in charge for all but a handful of the city's building projects. When budget problems brought the City Architect's Office to its knees in 1931 and again in 1944, he was shuttled back and forth between the architecture and engineering departments to assure that his salary and rank remained constant—a sure measure of his indispensability.[23]

Many of the city's building projects during the Depression were made possible by grants from the Public Works Administration (PWA) and the Works Progress Administration (WPA). The purpose of the relief programs was to provide temporary employment in the service of "worthwhile and socially desirable projects." Between 1934 and American entry into World War II in 1942, communities across the nation received funding for public buildings, schools, parks and recreation centers, sewer and water systems, and roadways. As an important population center, St. Paul was no exception.[24]

Were it not for these federal relief programs, Wigington's career could easily have halted at its peak. The City of St. Paul passed a number of bonding bills required for federal support of some of its larger projects but simply did not have the resources to fund the many types of buildings and structures that fell under the purview of the City Architect. Yet between 1934 and 1943 Wigington's name appeared on drawings for sixty city projects ranging from swimming pools to ice palaces.

The lion's share of Wigington's work during the Depression was taken up with park and playground structures. In 1927 the City of St. Paul owned and operated 33 playgrounds and was in the process of purchasing 18 more. But their development lagged behind the parks. While Como, Phalen, and Highland had been transformed into open-air community centers offering a multitude of activities, the playgrounds languished as little more than cleared squares with children's play equipment and a ball diamond. During the ensuing decade, the largest of the playgrounds sprouted the same variety of shelters and community buildings that had filled the parks in the 1910s and 1920s. Wigington designed a score of such buildings, beginning with a series of rustic playground shelters in 1934 and culminating in a majestic array of cut-stone community buildings at Hamline and Wilder playgrounds and Harriet Island Park. Designed in an austere variation of the Moderne style typical of the Depression era,

Cornerstone,
Hamline
Playground
Building

Don Wong, 2000

Rustic stone West
Minnehaha
Playground
Building, built 1937

Don Wong, 2000

Moderne-style
Hamline Playground
Building, built 1938

Don Wong, 2000

Main entrance,
Hamline Playground
Building

Don Wong, 2000

these buildings reflected the love of native materials and superior crafts-
manship typical of WPA projects.

One of Wigington's most enduring accomplishments under PWA and
WPA funding was the administration building at Holman Field, then St.
Paul's municipal airport. Between 1938 and 1940 more than $2 million in
federal funds and nearly half a million in city funds were poured into
development of the airport. Most of the work was done on the airfield
itself; built partially on swampland, it required enough sand to fill the
Empire State Building seven times over. The centerpiece was an administration building costing $250,000. In Wigington's design, cars were

housed beneath the main floor, in the first full basement to be built in an airport building. The roof boasted a promenade, allowing visitors a sweeping view of the airport and the city above. Walls of Kasota stone twenty inches thick were left hollow at the center for insulation. Claimed the airport director, "For fine workmanship, it will compare favorably with any building in Minnesota."[25]

The capstone of Wigington's career was a series of ice palaces created for the St. Paul Winter Carnival, each preceded by a set of elegant colored renderings. The city's winter carnival tradition, complete with ice castle, dated back to the winter of 1885–86, when St. Paul saw itself as the nation's next major metropolis. The carnival went on and a palace went up for two succeeding winters. But a variety of factors—economic, political, and meteorological—kept the tradition from being firmly established, despite restarts in 1896 and 1916. After the monumental successes of the 1880s, the city's business community was loath to take on the cost and engineering required for construction of a building doomed to melt at the first winter thaw.

Rising economic optimism near the end of the Depression—and a healthy infusion of WPA funds—revived the tradition in 1936–37. A great

The 1937 ice palace, the city's first in over fifty years, was a popular attraction.

Minnesota Historical Society

AMONG EQUALS

jagged enclosure of ice, half Norman castle keep, half Art Moderne structure, rose near the State Capitol, with Wigington in charge. For four of
the five ensuing winters, the ice palace tradition lived on. Wigington's
lavish Windsor Castle–inspired design was passed over in 1938, and warm
weather brought a hiatus in 1939. But he was back at the drawing board
in 1940, 1941, 1942 and 1947, designing castles for a succession of city
parks. Unseasonably warm weather in 1942 and 1947 halted construction
of the ice palaces before they were completed.[26]

Official recognition of Wigington's pivotal role in the operation of
the City Architect's Office finally arrived on November 11, 1942, when he
was named to a new position, architectural designer, created expressly
for him. The promotion turned out to be more a reflection of his past

*Seen from the top
of the Minnesota
State Capitol,
Wigington's ice
palace for the 1937
St. Paul Winter
Carnival towered
over surrounding
apartment buildings.*

*Minnesota Historical
Society*

Ice Palace, 1942
St. Paul Winter
Carnival. Northeast
elevation (pencil
and colored pencil
on tracing paper, 21˝
x 36˝; collection of
the City of St. Paul,
Department of
Technology and
Management
Services)

Warm weather halted construction of the 1942 ice palace
at the Highland Park Golf Course.

Minnesota Historical Society

accomplishments than a sign of new authority and responsibility, for he would never again have the opportunity to design a major public building.[27]

Less than a month after Wigington's promotion, the United States' entry into World War II brought a sudden end to the city's ambitious building programs. A few months later, in February 1943, the Works Progress Administration abruptly ended. At war's end, the City Architect's Office geared up again, but it never recovered the energy or scope of its years under Tewes and Bassford. Between 1946 and 1949, the year of Wigington's official retirement, the number of municipal projects under his signature declined dramatically. After more than twenty years in charge of the drafting office, he found himself working on such minutiae as a lunch counter for the Phalen Park Pavilion and a diving platform for the swimming dock. By the time he resigned in 1949, a significant new project had not crossed his desk for seven years. His years of service were recognized in a press release and at a departmental Christmas party in his honor, but a newspaper listing of a handful of his buildings was little more than an exercise in nostalgia for a governmental department whose years of glory had passed.[28]

As retirement approached, Wigington, at sixty-three still eager to work, assessed his future. Like other architects, he realized that the demand for new construction occasioned by returning GIs would create abundant opportunities for residential work. Intrigued by the kind of house plans coming out of California, he took leaves of absence to spend three successive winters there beginning in 1946–47. While in California he studied styles and trends in West Coast residential design and explored the possibility of doing design work for private up-scale homebuilders in Los Angeles. Wigington's research might have proven influential on homes he designed for two leading St. Paul businessmen, Jack G. Butwin and Simon Klein. The Butwin home, a four-level house constructed in 1948 at a cost of $40,000, was modestly detailed on the exterior, even by the bland standards of post-war construction. But the house securely commands both frontages of its corner site, and its floor plan, encompassing 3,000 square feet, still appears contemporary after fifty years.[29]

Jack G. Butwin
House, St. Paul,
built 1948. The gable
over the entry was
added by a later
owner.

Don Wong, 2000

Wigington's correspondence suggests that health problems were the main impetus for his final departure from the City Architect's Office. First tendered at the end of 1948 as an extended sick leave, his resignation became official late in the summer of 1949. On August 29 he left the office for the last time and began preparations for a move to California. After short visits with their daughters in Omaha and Kansas City, Clarence and Viola arrived at their winter apartment in Los Angeles in early November.[30]

With neither state credentials nor a prospective clientele in California, Wigington balked at giving up his Minnesota practice altogether. During his extended sick leave, he had simultaneously applied for membership

Plans and
perspective drawing,
House No. 2671, 1953
(ink and pencil on
vellum, 14˝ x 17 3/8˝;
Wigington Papers,
Northwest
Architectural
Archives, University
of Minnesota
Libraries)

in the St. Paul Chapter of the American Institute of Architects (AIA) and begun to inquire about transferring his registration as an architect to California. He had been registered in Minnesota since 1937, but this was not sufficient for the senior classification he sought in California. As the leading architectural association in the country, the AIA, he thought,

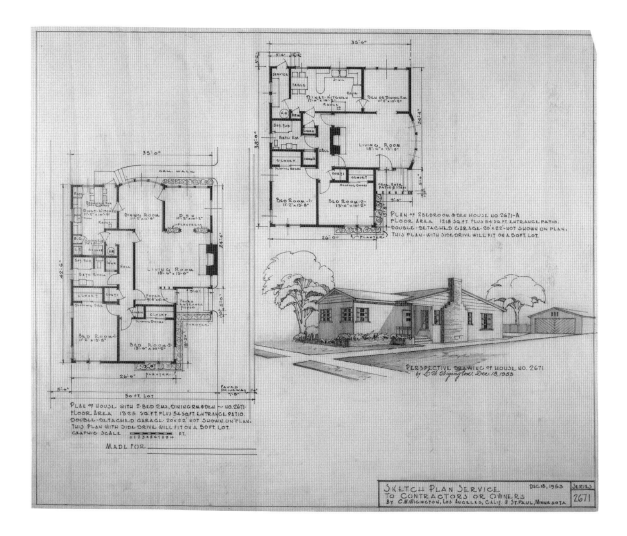

would afford him the professional affiliation he needed to give his extensive architectural experience its appropriate weight.[31]

During his ultimately unsuccessful effort to achieve registration as a senior architect in California, he maintained the semblance of a St. Paul office at 561 Aurora Avenue. Managed by his brother, architectural designer Paul Wigington, it functioned as little more than an address for a letterhead to which Clarence could append the very important phrase "Registered Architect."

For all his woes with the California registration procedure, Los Angeles quickly became Wigington's year-round home. His initial intention to spend six months of the year in each office never came to fruition. For the next eight years Wigington devoted his architectural energies to his small practice in southern California. His 1955 letterhead identified him as an "industrial designer," but a list of projects he enumerated ten years later included three Masonic lodges, five churches, and several private residences as well as a handful of small commercial buildings.[32]

In the meantime, Wigington maintained close personal ties with relatives and former colleagues in St. Paul. Perhaps it was the pull of those old connections that led him to spend his final active professional years in his old terrain. In late 1957 or early 1958, he moved his St. Paul office to the Hamm Building as the first step in his return to the city. By September 1958 Clarence and Viola were settled into a Dayton Avenue residence and Wigington began the last phase of his career, working in semiretirement on a handful of modest projects in St. Paul and Minneapolis. His last known commission was a remodeling of the St. Paul AAA Clubhouse in 1962. Three years later, on the recommendation of pre-eminent local architect Bruce Abrahamson, he was awarded life membership as a Professional Associate in the St. Paul Chapter of the AIA. This honor brought his name before the public one last time.[33]

Full retirement came in the spring of 1963, when the Wigingtons followed their California winter with a move to Kansas City to live with their daughter Muriel and her family. Yet even on the cusp of his eighties, it was difficult for Wigington to acknowledge that his career was over. In a letter to his brother Paul, he lamented the decision to move in with his daughter, claiming that he was still capable of supporting himself and his wife. When his sister Hazel died in 1966, he initially leaped at the opportunity to return to St. Paul to live with her husband, Dr. Albert Butler. But poor health intervened and he remained in Kansas City. One year later, on July 7, 1967, he died while still living with his daughter.[34]

Wigington in the 1940s

Minnesota Historical Society

Ice Throne, 1940
Sketch, undated
Pencil and colored pencil on tracing paper
11.75″ x 12.5″

Collection of the City of St. Paul,
Department of Technology and Management Services

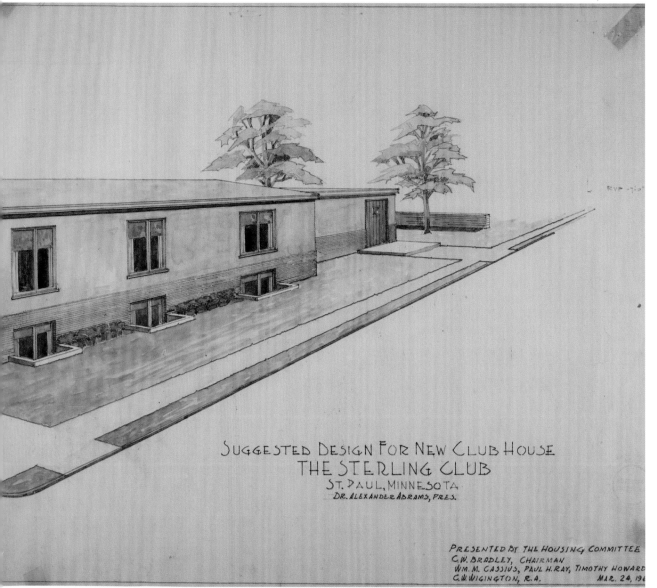

SUGGESTED DESIGN FOR NEW CLUB HOUSE
THE STERLING CLUB
ST. PAUL, MINNESOTA
DR. ALEXANDER ABRAMS, PRES.

PRESENTED BY THE HOUSING COMMITTEE
C.W. BRADLEY, CHAIRMAN
WM. M. CASSIUS, PAUL H. RAY, TIMOTHY HOWARD
C.W. WIGINGTON, R.A.   MAR. 24, 196_

The Sterling Club, "Suggested Design for New Club House," 1962
Blueline, hand-colored with pencil
14″ x 33″

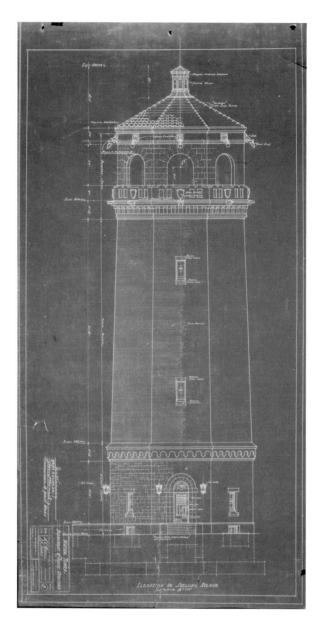

Highland Park Water Tower, 1927
West (Snelling Avenue) elevation
Blueprint (no. 5 of 15 sheets)
36″ x 24″

Minnesota Historical Society

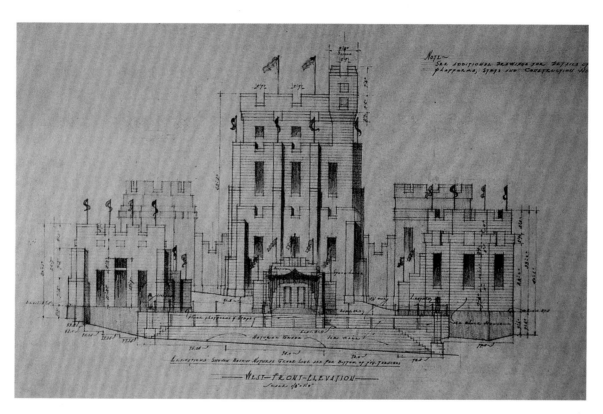

Ice Palace, 1940 St. Paul Winter Carnival
West front elevation
Pencil and colored pencil on vellum
21″ x 35″

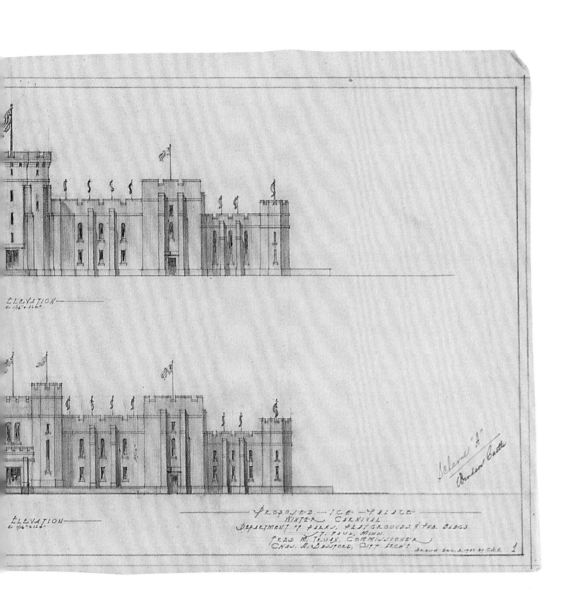

ELEVATION
¼"=1'-0"

ELEVATION
¼"=1'-0"

Scheme "1"
Windsor Castle

PROPOSED ICE PALACE
WINTER CARNIVAL
DEPARTMENT OF PARKS, PLAYGROUNDS & PUB. BLDGS
ST. PAUL, MINN.
FRED M. TRUAX, COMMISSIONER
CHAS. A. BASSFORD, CITY ARCH'T.
Drawn Dec. 9, 1937 by C.M.B.

1

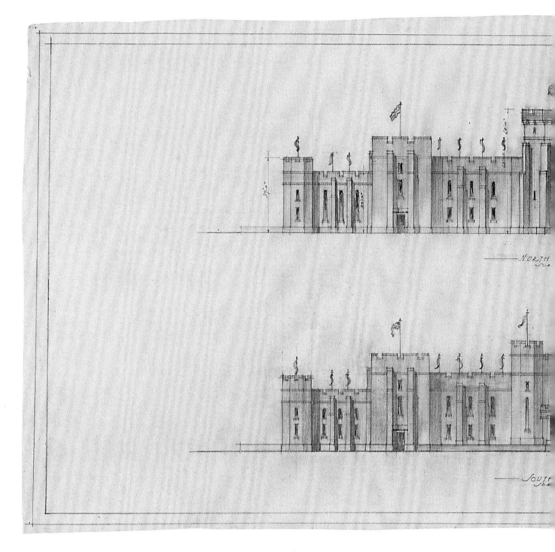

Ice Palace, 1938 St. Paul Winter Carnival
"Scheme A, Windsor Castle" (design not selected)
North and south elevations
Pencil and colored pencil on tracing paper
15″ x 35″

Collection of the City of St. Paul,
Department of Technology and Management Services

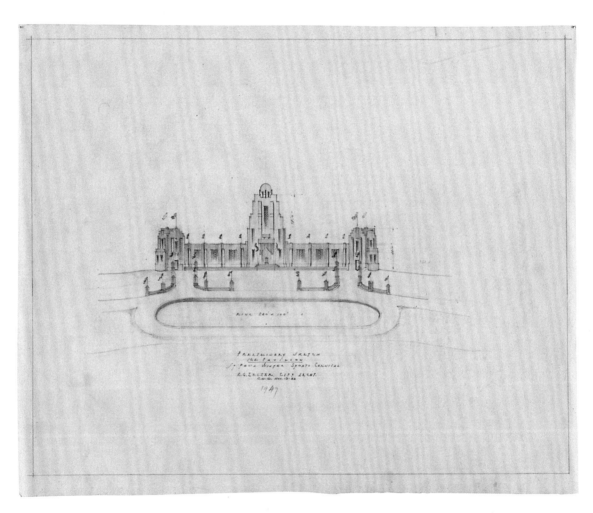

Ice Pavilion, 1947 St. Paul Winter Carnival
Preliminary sketch, 1946
Pencil and colored pencil on vellum
15″ x 18″

Collection of the City of St. Paul,
Department of Technology and Management Services

3

A STRONGER SOUL WITHIN
A FINER FRAME

C LARENCE WIGINGTON'S eighty-four years spanned one of the most dynamic periods in American social history. Born six years after the formal end of southern Reconstruction in 1877, he lived through the imposition of racial segregation and social separation in American life sanctioned by the 1896 U.S. Supreme Court decision *Plessy v. Ferguson*. He was seventy-one years old in 1954 when the Supreme Court reversed its earlier decision, ruling that, in the case of education, racial segregation was deleterious and harmful. He was eighty when the Reverend Martin Luther King addressed the nation during the March on Washington. He lived to see the passage of the Civil Rights Act of 1964 and the Voting Rights Act of 1965 but died before passage of the Civil Rights Act of 1968, a by-product of King's assassination and the widespread civil disobedience that followed.

During Wigington's formative years, two African American leaders espousing dichotomous philosophies about the proper role of African Americans in American life debated issues that would profoundly affect his future. Booker T. Washington, an educator and the founder of the Tuskegee Institute, insisted that young blacks would be better served in American society by acquiring a vocational skill, working hard, and engaging in entrepreneurial activities designed to produce wealth. He believed that agitating for social and political equality, under the strictures of prevailing attitudes, would only serve to heighten racial animosity. It was acquired wealth and respectability, Washington maintained, that would lead naturally to political rights and social acceptability.

Harvard-trained scholar W. E. B. Du Bois, on the other hand, was an advocate for full social, economic, and political integration of the African American into American life, predicting that the future of the country in the twentieth century would be directly related to its ability to transcend the stigma of color and racism. He reasoned that without political rights for blacks, there was no guarantee of economic parity. He also advocated college training for African American youths as preparation for leadership so desperately needed by the race, suggesting that at least ten percent—the Talented Tenth, as he called them—be enrolled in American colleges and universities.

During the summer of 1902, as Wigington was beginning his architectural apprenticeship in Omaha, the Afro-American Council, then the country's leading African American civil rights organization, met in St. Paul. At that fateful meeting, delegates preferring political activism and those supporting Washington's more accommodating position on the race issue clashed over control of the council. In this first test of Washington's political strength, his forces prevailed; he would continue to exert influence over African Americans through the first decade of the century. But the schism within the council deepened, leading to its eventual demise, and the popularity of Washington's philosophy gradually waned after his death in 1915.[1]

Like African American leaders elsewhere, those in St. Paul were divided over the issue of accommodation versus political activism. Some of these men and women had attended educational institutions established during Reconstruction primarily to train African Americans. They were vocal in their opposition to policies that promoted racial separation, disenfranchisement, and discriminatory practices in public accommodations, employment, and educational opportunities. Between 1889 and 1910 they founded, endorsed, or established chapters of organizations created in part to safeguard their civil and political rights in Minnesota. While revering Washington and his work, they chose to pursue the avenue of protest.[2]

John Quincy
Adams, editor of
The Appeal, was
among Wigington's
mentors.

*Minnesota Historical
Society*

Wigington's decision to move to St. Paul in 1914 brought him to the right place at the right time. There he found a cadre of African American leaders who not only welcomed him into the community's social order but also began grooming him for leadership. Among his new mentors were the editor of *The Appeal*, John Quincy Adams; attorneys William R. Morris and William T. Francis; Doctors Val Do Turner and James H. Redd; the Reverends A. H. Lealtad and Stephen L. Theobald, clergymen of St. Philip's Episcopal Church and St. Peter Claver Catholic Church, respectively; and community activists Mrs. Nellie Francis, Mrs. T. H. Lyles, and Orrington C. Hall. It did not take long for Wigington to demonstrate his own capacity for leadership.[3]

On April 6, 1917, the United States formally entered World War I. As in other military conflicts, African Americans endeavored to volunteer their services individually and collectively in a demonstration of patriotism. And just as before, the U.S. government at first refused to induct them into the armed services, then established segregated African American units led primarily by white officers.

To augment the country's armed forces, state National Guard units were called into federal service. Historically, they too had refused to enlist African Americans. Fear of possible insurrection by armed and militarily trained African Americans, who were patriotic but politically disenfranchised, challenged even the sensibilities of northern white liberals. Upon declaration of war against Germany, only two states—Illinois and New York—moved to accept African Americans in their National Guard units.

Prevented by the prevailing social convention from enlisting in the Minnesota National Guard, Wigington sought opportunities for himself and other African American males to support the war effort. He turned

16th Battalion of
the Minnesota
Home Guard, 1918,
in an incomplete
panorama; detail
at right

James Griffin

his attention to the Minnesota Home Guard, which, in the absence of the National Guard, had been organized in April 1917 by the newly formed Minnesota Commission of Public Safety to protect the home front. Made up of citizens not likely to be conscripted, the Home Guard would soon number twenty-three battalions with more than 8,000 men.[4]

Sometime during March or April of 1918, Wigington petitioned Governor J. A. A. Burnquist to form a separate battalion of the Minnesota Home Guard for African American citizens. He may have been encouraged in this effort by many of his mentors—Adams, Lealtad, Francis, Turner, Lyles, and others—who were board members of St. Paul's NAACP chapter. Fortuitously, Governor Burnquist was then president of the chapter and Turner was chairman of its board of directors.

The petition provided Governor Burnquist with an unexpected opportunity for national leadership on this race issue. At the time most Minnesotans were very accepting of social separation between the races; de facto segregation was a way of life. *Plessy v. Ferguson* had made it legally possible to codify that relationship. Though Governor Burnquist was active in the NAACP, he recognized the political folly of directly confronting an accepted cultural norm. Wigington's proposal for a separate African American battalion created a win-win situation for the governor. In a critical election year, he could use his executive powers to create a "separate but equal" battalion of African Americans, thus satisfying African American voters without offending his white constituency.[5]

CAP WIGINGTON

Appointed captain of the 16th Battalion's Company A, Wigington (standing, right) was promptly nicknamed "Cap."

James Griffin

On April 20 the *Twin City Star* reported that the governor and the adjutant general of the State of Minnesota had ordered immediate establishment of the 16th Battalion of the Minnesota Home Guard. Companies A and B formed in St. Paul; approximately two weeks later, companies C and D formed in Minneapolis. At the same time, Dr. Turner received permission from the governor to establish a medical corps to serve the 16th Battalion. In all, about 400 men would enroll.[6]

The notion of belonging to the Home Guard met with immediate popularity in African American communities. They organized dances and other social activities as fund raisers in support of their black militiamen. Accompanied by a newly formed band and drum and bugle corps, the companies of the 16th Battalion took part in public parades and exhibition drills. For his leadership in organizing the battalion, Clarence Wigington was commissioned captain of Company A. He would affectionately be known ever after by the nickname "Cap."[7]

Wigington's leadership was critical to this concession from the state's political leaders. A Republican, he was sagacious enough to acquire what he wanted without alienating the party leadership or appearing to have accepted the status quo. He was roundly praised for integrating the state's militia, even if on a de facto segregated basis.[8]

"Separate but equal" characterized more than life in the military. An entrenched system of social separation had long existed in the Twin Cities. Blacks and whites may have lived in close proximity to one another, attended public schools together, and even worked shoulder to shoulder, but their cultural and religious lives remained a world apart. Unwelcome in white civic, social, and fraternal organizations, and discouraged from using restaurants and hotels for social functions, blacks in the Twin Cities wove their own rich tapestry of organizations and activities.

Clarence and Viola Wigington were at the core of the St. Paul black community's social set. Their light complexions made them welcome

St. Anthony Avenue was home to many of St. Paul's prominent black families, including *Appeal* editor John Quincy Adams, who lived in this elaborate Queen Anne house.

Minnesota Historical Society

among those to whom color gradients were important. In addition, Clarence's education and occupation set his family apart; his income placed them in the top ten percent of black families nationally. They lived in a racially mixed neighborhood and worshipped at St. Philip's Episcopal Church, a congregation of largely well-educated and progressive black parishioners.

After Wigington secured employment with the city in 1915, the family moved from his brother's home to a house at 582 Rondo Avenue. Several moves followed. By 1922 he was affluent enough to purchase a spacious twin home at 679 St. Anthony Avenue, then one of the better residential streets in St. Paul. There he set up an office in an upstairs bedroom, where he often worked late into the night on architectural projects.[9]

Family life in this home was comfortable and decidedly upper-middle-class. The area where the Wigingtons lived, west of Dale Street, was known in the black community as Oatmeal Hill, meant to suggest the wholesome diet of more affluent northern blacks. The cream of St. Paul's black society lived in these substantial, well-maintained homes. East of Dale Street was "Cornmeal Valley," a neighborhood of blighted housing on lower St. Anthony, Rondo, and Carroll avenues, where blacks with more limited incomes and education lived.[10]

Daughter Muriel recalls Wigington as a good father, providing all of their material needs but, given his responsibilities, often too busy to spend much time with his children. He encouraged both daughters to study art and music, areas where he himself demonstrated considerable talent. Muriel describes their mother, Viola, as an excellent cook, talented seamstress, inveterate bridge player, movie afficionado, and voracious newspaper reader who was her husband's verbal equal. Granddaughter Gayle

A STRONGER SOUL

Pemberton characterizes Viola, and other women in her family, as "independent of spirit, mind, opinion, belief, and emotion." The Wigingtons entertained often, hosting dinner parties for friends, community leaders, and out-of-town guests. They also were part of a large extended family, traveling frequently to Kansas and Nebraska to visit relatives. Over the course of Clarence's career, four of his siblings—Paul, Clifford, Hazel, and Birdie—would move to St. Paul, all living in close proximity to one another.[11]

The Wigington grandchildren fondly remember visits to the house on St. Anthony Avenue. Gayle Pemberton describes her older sister's ability to charm their indulgent grandfather: "Papa . . . would take a break from his boardwork and amble hand-in-hand with [Carolyn] to the corner candy store. Once there, he would point to a Fudgsicle or candy bar and ask her, 'Do you want one of those?' Her standard reply was 'I want two, Papa!' and two she would get." Michael Bohanon recalls the detached garage and large backyard where his grandfather loved to putter. The garage housed his automobiles, primarily Oldsmobiles and Buicks, and Wigington was as fastidious in their upkeep as he was in his own appearance. Bohanon's visits often ended in one of those cars, where he and his grandfather would sit listening to baseball games.[12]

Wigington family in about 1924. From left: Muriel, Viola, Clarence, and Mildred.

Carolyn Pemberton

For prominent citizens like the Wigingtons, opportunities for community involvement abounded. African American political clubs, usually organized around the candidacy of a particular politician, were customarily open to any black male. Fraternal organizations, lodges, and women's auxiliaries also were gender specific, usually with admission requirements. Social and civic clubs reflected the social stratification within the black community; membership in many of them was limited and highly sought after.

Together, Clarence and Viola joined the Forty Club, a popular couples' club founded in the early 1920s. He was a member of a Masonic order, serving a term as Exalted Ruler of Gopher Lodge No. 105, Improved Benevolent Protective Order of Elks of the World. And she belonged to several women's clubs and tea circles. Clarence also was a charter member of the Sterling Club, a men's club that quickly became one of the leading social clubs in Twin Cities black communities; Viola joined the women's auxiliary. Founded in 1918, the Sterling Club counted on its rolls professional men, white-collar workers, and railway workers. Wigington was elected to the first board of directors and served as vice president in 1925. He also designed the clubhouse, built in 1924. Wigington would remain a club member for forty-three years; when he died in 1967, he was the last surviving charter member.[13]

Though he was widely respected in his public and professional life, Wigington's home life proved somewhat less exemplary. In 1932, after

The Forty Club,
a black couples'
group founded in
the 1920s, gathered
for a 1948 picnic.

John Banks photo,
Minnesota Historical
Society

Muriel's marriage, Viola left Clarence, taking Mildred, who was then in her third year of college, to California to live with cousins. "Nana had decided to leave Papa, tired of his verbal abusiveness and profligacy," Gayle Pemberton explained. "Papa got his pay regularly, but didn't bring home enough of it, and was occasionally waylaid by card games and flashy women." At least one affair was widely known in the community but did not seem to compromise his public image. Apparently, some reconciliation took place in 1937, when Viola returned to Minnesota.[14]

Despite his prominent position in St. Paul's black community—and regardless of any troubles at home—Wigington apparently was not invited to join two of the most socially prominent organizations for black men: the T.S.T.C. and the Omicron Boule of Sigma Pi Phi Fraternity. Founded in 1896, the T.S.T.C. (Twelve Solid Together Club) was an exclusive group

Mother's Day, 1939: (back row) Clarence, Viola holding grandson Michael Bohanon, and daughter Mildred Bohanon; (front row) daughter Muriel Wigington and son-in-law M. Leo Bohanon. Clarence and Muriel wear carnations honoring their mothers.

Carolyn Pemberton

of twelve men who gathered for a dinner meeting once a month in the homes of its members to discuss pressing issues of the day. Elaborate formal announcements were mailed and formal attire required for each meeting. The club also hosted social affairs for which invitations were coveted. Although the Wigingtons were included in these events, there is no record of Clarence being invited to join or refusing membership.[15]

The Sigma Pi Phi Fraternity, founded in 1904, was the first African American Greek letter fraternity in the country. Membership, open to African American men of attainment and refinement, required completion of at least a baccalaureate degree. This organization was the embodiment of Du Bois's Talented Tenth. In 1922 ten Twin Cities men chartered the fraternity's fifteenth chapter, the Omicron Boule. Wigington was not among them, nor was he invited to join during his lifetime. Clearly, his career accomplishments placed him on par with other inductees, who included such close associates as Rev. Theobald, Dr. Turner, Gayle Hilyer, and William Morris. His exclusion may simply have been because his art instruction and architectural apprenticeship did not constitute baccalaureate training.[16]

Wigington found other ways to make his mark on the community: he began devoting his energy and leadership skills to organizations dedicated to ameliorating the condition of African Americans. Conservative by nature, Wigington avoided those organizations that represented the radical fringes of the protest tradition, such as the Universal Negro Improvement Association, founded by Marcus Garvey, whose flamboyant rhetoric most of the established African American leadership rejected. Nor did Wigington sympathize with a fledgling communist/socialist movement that attempted to establish itself in St. Paul's black community in the 1930s.[17]

Instead, he chose to champion the cause of social justice for African Americans in employment and other arenas through involvement in two more mainstream organizations, the Urban League and the NAACP. Of the two organizations, less is known about his involvement with the NAACP. Although a member, he did not appear to take a leadership role.

It may have been because the organization sought remedies to complex racial problems through protracted and expensive litigation—still a radical notion for the era.[18]

Wigington's involvement with the Urban League went deeper, explained perhaps by his affinity for the simplicity of its mission: to secure employment opportunities for African Americans and extend much-needed social services to the black community. The National Urban League had been founded in New York City in 1910 to address the growing need among migrants from the rural South for housing, employment, education, and health services as they acclimated to their new urban environment. A board of both African American and white directors guided the organization.[19]

Blacks arriving in Minnesota in the 1910s faced the same challenges as those in eastern cities. Local employers, fearing the influx of African Americans experienced by Chicago and Detroit, refused to hire black workers, often requiring them to show proof of residency that predated the mass migration. Restrictive housing covenants and persistent housing discrimination created overcrowded conditions in low-income neighborhoods, fostering unhealthful environments. But the new arrivals did not have the benefit of community-based agencies to help them.

At first, assistance came from African American leaders who used their contacts in the white community to secure employment and housing for the newcomers. Larger African American churches such as Pilgrim Baptist and St. James A.M.E. also stepped in to help. In the 1920s the cause was taken up by newly established African American community centers like the Phyllis Wheatley House in Minneapolis and the Hallie Q. Brown House in St. Paul, which attempted to address housing and health issues. But even their combined efforts could not meet the growing need.[20]

In 1923 a group of concerned African American citizens approached the St. Paul Community Chest, a citywide social service agency funded in part by philanthropic giving, to request support for a full-time employee who would address the problem. Because they were not formally affiliated with an agency, their request was denied. Undeterred, several members of the group who knew of the Urban League's work in New York extended an invitation for a league representative to visit St. Paul. The result: organization of a Twin Cities branch in 1923, patterned on the national league with a board of white and African American directors. At the outset, the league was denounced by the Chamber of Commerce, which feared its existence would only encourage more black migration to the Twin Cities, thus fueling racial tensions. African American leaders convincingly pointed out that such problems already existed, that future migration

was inevitable, and that the community needed a program to address the issues.[21]

Wigington played a key role in the Urban League during its formative years, a period during which the St. Paul and Minneapolis branches operated jointly for efficiency. While a full-time St. Paul city employee, he also served part-time as the league's executive secretary, a position equivalent to chief executive officer, which he held from 1932 to 1938. In October 1937 the *Minneapolis Spokesman* noted the reorganization of the St. Paul Urban League; the next year Clarence N. Mitchell, a professional social worker, was hired as its full-time executive secretary. Wigington continued to serve the organization as a board member between 1941 and 1947. In 1947 he was named board president, perhaps the first African American to serve in that capacity.[22]

In 1941 the St. Paul Urban League published a pamphlet entitled *You May Quote Us on This!*, designed to inform the public about the Urban League's origins and its work. In the publication Wigington addressed the issue, "Do Negroes Face Any Problems in Getting Jobs in Tax-Supported Institutions?" He wrote:

> Like all other citizens, Negroes wish to be treated fairly when they take civil service examinations and when they seek employment in tax-supported institutions. Sometimes they are given such treatment, but the cases of discrimination against them because of race occur with uncomfortable frequency.[23]

Wigington was well aware of discrimination within the civil service system. Working from an office in City Hall, he interacted daily with councilmen and city commissioners, often lobbying informally for employment opportunities for blacks. And when he heard of position openings, he used his influence to secure employment for them. He also brought news of employment opportunities to community forums sponsored by the NAACP and Urban League in the late 1930s. Held at the Hallie Q. Brown Community Center, the meetings served to promote discussion about black employment and document instances of employment discrimination.[24]

In 1939 Wigington and the Urban League's Mitchell joined forces to encourage African American men to take the civil service examination for St. Paul's police and fire departments. Racial animosities ran strong in both departments; between 1920 and 1937, no black men were appointed to the force. Yet Wigington's own success with the civil service system spurred him to urge others to try. He and Mitchell conducted workshops to familiarize candidates with the exam and help them improve their knowledge in subject areas on the test.[25]

More than 1,100 men, including thirty blacks, registered for the police and fire department's civil service examination in 1939. But lingering effects of the Depression and the onset of World War II kept positions from being filled until 1941. Among the first African Americans from that group to be appointed to the police force was James Griffin, Wigington's godson. Griffin went on to a distinguished career in law enforcement; in 1972 he was appointed St. Paul's first black deputy chief of police.[26]

Wigington's influence and leadership reached far beyond the African American community. Builders and contractors throughout the Twin Cities sought his professional advice and frequently called on him to address their business meetings. He was appointed special civil service examiner in the area of architecture for both St. Paul and Minneapolis. And in 1948 Governor Luther W. Youngdahl named him to the newly established Selective Service Board for Ramsey County.[27]

In his capacity as an Urban League board member, Wigington may have helped facilitate the work of several government commissions on racial issues during the 1940s. The Governor's Interracial Commission of Minnesota, established in the aftermath of the Detroit Riot of 1943, was created by Governor Edward J. Thye to explore Minnesota's racial climate. Among the commission's thirteen charter members was S. Vincent Owens, executive secretary of the St. Paul Urban League, who, with the endorsement of his own board, pledged assistance from the Urban League in the form of office space and staff support. Around 1945, in his capacity as a member of the League's board, Wigington was undoubtedly involved in the Twin Cities Council for Permanent Fair Employment

Practices Commission, part of a nationwide effort to pass congressional legislation aimed at eliminating discrimination in employment practices.[28]

Wigington's organizational affiliations extended to California as well. One membership was primarily social. After moving to Los Angeles, Clarence and Viola joined the Minnesota Club, made up of "exiles from the frozen North living out their days among the palms," as Gayle Pemberton recalls it. They all brought their visiting grandchildren to the club's annual picnics. "My grandparents were crack bridge players," writes Pemberton, "and I remember that card tables proliferated among the wooden picnic tables. . . . I was a very young child among retirees. I was also distinctly brown among the fair."[29]

In 1950 Wigington was asked to reactivate the California Chapter of the National Technical Association (NTA). Made up of architects, engineers, chemists, and draftsmen, the NTA was organized in Chicago in 1926. The purpose of the NTA was "the collection and dissemination of information concerning the opportunities of Negroes in the technical and engineering fields; the aid and encouragement of the Negro youth in preparation for these fields; the advancement of science and engineering in all of their branches; the promotion of the interests of the profession among the darker races, and the breaking down of barriers in the profession due to race prejudice."[30]

Because there were not enough trained professionals in Minnesota to constitute a chapter, Wigington had affiliated with the NTA through its Chicago chapter. He continued that association for so many years that he jokingly referred to himself as "the dean of Negro architects in this country." The task of reactivating the Los Angeles chapter had fallen to him as Western Region vice president, a position to which he was appointed by NTA president Donald F. White in 1950.[31]

A dated membership list in hand, Wigington enlisted the support of a small group of Californians including Paul Gomez, Joseph S. Dunning, Titus Alexander, James H. Garrott, John T. Riddell, Roy Sealey, and Paul R. Williams. Wigington developed a particularly close relationship with Williams, the architect of numerous celebrated homes in Hollywood. On

A man of gentle
persuasion, not
open confrontation

*St. Paul Dispatch-Pioneer
Press photo, Minnesota
Historical Society*

the strength of that friendship, he persuaded Williams to serve as chapter president. In a letter to the new NTA president, Calvin L. McKissack, Wigington expressed satisfaction in having revitalized the Los Angeles chapter and offered the organization his services by traveling to San Francisco, Oakland, Portland, and Seattle to recruit new members for the Western Region.[32]

Throughout his thirty-five-year career, both in Minnesota and as a California transplant, the focus of Wigington's civic life had remained simple: to advance the economic well-being of African Americans through education, employment, and housing. He pursued this not with empty rhetoric or open confrontation but through reasoned dialogue and structured programs, leveraging his considerable influence to aid those with no individual or collective voice.

Cap Wigington, 1940s

St. Paul Pioneer Press

4

ARCHITECTURAL LEGACY

ANY CAREER covering nearly four decades of the twentieth century marches over a significant amount of architectural terrain. Even the design of civic and institutional buildings, those bastions of architectural conservatism, undergoes transformation over so long a period. Between 1915 and 1945 sober Roman temples were replaced by picturesque reminders of English university education; these in turn gave way to civic monuments with heroic overtones but few historical resonances. Park buildings, the last vestige of the nineteenth-century fad for rusticity in the city, also metamorphosed into minimonuments of stone, each exhibiting the style then at the height of public favor.

Throughout Wigington's tenure in the St. Paul City Architect's Office, the city building programs were a barometer of national tastes and styles. Wigington and his peers worked to keep pace with the shifts in fashion. As they discovered, staying in style was a continuous education, for no turn-of-the-century schooling could fully equip an architect to deal with the sea changes in American architecture that the 1930s would bring. These profound changes form the national context within which all of Wigington's work must be assessed.

The most local of contexts, the City Architect's Office itself, also had a profound effect on the design process. During his many years in the office, Wigington worked in an intensely collegial atmosphere. Several of his co-workers were among his closest friends, and many of the larger projects brought as many as five draftsmen to the same drawing and fifteen to the project as a whole. His work was thus never detached from the contributions of others.

How, then, are we to define and illumine Wigington's unique contribution? Like most architects of his period, Wigington cared little about implanting a personal signature on his work. It was enough for him to master the technical aspects of design and construction and understand the style appropriate for the building at hand. Yet he entered the City Architect's Office with a certain direction, a certain way of looking at possible design solutions, already implanted on his architectural consciousness. The tension between these two poles—Wigington in context and Wigington as an individual—informs much of the discussion that follows.

Wigington's Omaha years provide two clues to the way he would conceive of buildings throughout his career. First, he cut his teeth as an architect on the pared-down Gothicism of his Omaha mentor, Thomas Kimball. Several elements of the late English Gothic look—agitated skylines, martially ordered wall openings, dramatic specimen windows, and great, flat wall surfaces—infused the practice of Kimball and became Wigington's forte as well. Gothicism itself, even in its altered, late English form, never dominated Wigington's buildings; even his churches were more neoclassical than Gothic. But he inherited from Kimball an understanding of buildings as a sequence of shallowly ornamented planes with articulated upper edges—an architectural device that transferred easily from style to style, building type to building type.

Second, Wigington's emergence as an architect coincided with the ascent of neoclassicism in American architecture. However Gothic his method of surface composition might be, he drew most of his building elements from Renaissance precedents. Horizontal parapets, not spires, terminated his towers, and some kind of classical screen or portico, however contorted the form, found its way onto the façades of numerous designs throughout his career. His design for the street façade of Omaha's Zion Baptist Church presented a trove of geometrical motifs, all of vaguely Renaissance parentage, that he would return to again and again—shallow triangles suggesting

All Saints Parish House in Omaha exhibits the pared-down Gothicism favored by Wigington's mentor Thomas Kimball.

Bostwick-Frohardt Collection, owned by KMTV, on permanent loan to Western Heritage Museum, Omaha, Nebraska

The façade of Zion Baptist Church, built 1913, reveals architectural motifs that Wigington returned to throughout his career.

Paul Clifford Larson, 1999

Strong central windows, like these on the Broomfield and Crutchfield Apartments, built 1913, became hallmarks of Wigington's style.

Omaha City Planning Department, 1982

gables, segmented curves suggesting vaults, vertical runs of projecting brick suggesting columns and pilasters.

Most of Wigington's residential work in Omaha was indistinguishable, at least on the exterior, from pattern-book architecture. Clients who wanted a bungalow got a product without frills or even any particular singularity. But several multifamily dwellings and one complete church design brought Wigington's youthful skills and design predilections to the fore. The identical, award-winning Broomfield and Crutchfield duplexes are a case in point. At first glance simple rectangles in a Craftsman vein, they pierce the skyline with a succession of minutely scaled triangles and rectangles—a sort of Gothicism shorn of religious aspirations. Their one bit of surface contouring is a framing element setting off the pair of windows above the entry. The device is classical in detail—four pilasters rise from a broad pedestal—but pure Wigington in the eccentricity of its execution. His fondness for strong, central elaborations, regardless of their function, would be a hallmark of his designs for the City of St. Paul. One can always sense him looking for that one element of the building to put on center stage and wrap with scenic effects, whatever the dictates of stylistic propriety.

For the façade of Como Park Elementary School—the first city project that can be attributed with some assurance to Wigington—he implanted a classical screen on the building, giving it a sense of ceremony utterly foreign to the Mediterranean sunniness of its Randolph Heights School model. The screen of columns embraces administrative offices as well as the entry, suggesting a center of serious purpose in a building otherwise suffused with air and light.

The classical idealism of the Como Park school carried over to Homecroft School as well. The first entire building with which Wigington can properly be credited, Homecroft is unique among his school designs for the utter severity of its skyline and the subordination of the central entry to projecting bays at the ends. These bays are set off by gables and elaborated with arched openings, drawn upward into a pair of long windows illuminating the staircases. The eight-room plan devised for this school

served as a model for the more mildly detailed Groveland Park School that came from Eisenmenger's desk
a few years later.

Homecroft would be the last St. Paul school to
display such neoclassical elements as columns and
shallow gables. Avant garde as it was in its modular
planning, its historical dress was rapidly going out of
style. Since the first decade of the twentieth century,
a new fashion in school building had been sweeping
the country. Loosely based on English universities
dating to the early Renaissance, it came to be known
as Collegiate Gothic. Apart from its visual appeal, the rationale for the style
was obvious: its historic associations with the most revered seats of learn-
ing in the English-speaking world.

St. Paul's Central High School of 1912, designed by State Architect
Clarence Johnston, was a masterpiece of Collegiate Gothic. The style
allowed the school building to be planned around purely functional
requirements, then imposed a system for organizing the surface and apply-
ing ornament that gave the building its artistic signature. But the City
Architect's Office was slow to adopt the style in buildings generated by its
own employees. Even after Collegiate Gothic elements were tentatively
grafted onto Groveland Park School in 1920, city draftsmen continued to
dabble for years with an uninspired eclecticism that seemed to owe more
to factory design than currents in school architecture.

The turning point came in 1924 when Wigington replaced Eisenmenger
as the primary architect of school buildings. Coincidental or not, the year
he took charge, Collegiate Gothic arrived in all its glory. First to be planned
and built in the style were Woodrow Wilson Junior High School and its
clone, John Marshall Senior High. Their Collegiate Gothic elements—a
towering entry bay and regular piercing of the parapet with downspouts—
fed Wigington's craving for pictorial effects and punctuated skylines. Horizontal bands of stone wrap the massive corner bays, and, in the buildings'
strongest ornamental flourish, elaborate carving above the door suggests

an arcade of Gothic tracery. With Central High School now entombed in a concrete remodeling, Marshall and Wilson schools are the best remaining examples of Collegiate Gothic built with city money.

Washington High School and Monroe Junior High followed in short order. The design for the façade of Monroe has been all but obliterated by a one-story addition, but even successive stripping of decorative detail from Washington has failed to rob it of its powerful entryway and the proliferation of linear ornament that marked Wigington's interpretation of the Collegiate Gothic style.

While local scholastic design began to settle around a single plan and appearance, park building design became even more diverse than it had been in the eclecticism of the 1910s. In Wigington's hands, however, each style seemed to be chosen for a reason. The park shelters at Battle Creek were wrought with the kind of log-and-boulder rusticism that befit a setting as close to wilderness as anything in the city limits. At the other extreme, Highland Park gained a water tower that reflected the sunny skies and fair weather of the Mediterranean; even in winter months it seems to speak of warmer climes.

ARCHITECTURAL LEGACY

Identical designs for Woodrow Wilson Junior High School and John Marshall
Senior High School, built 1924, give full expression to the Collegiate Gothic style.

Don Wong, 2000

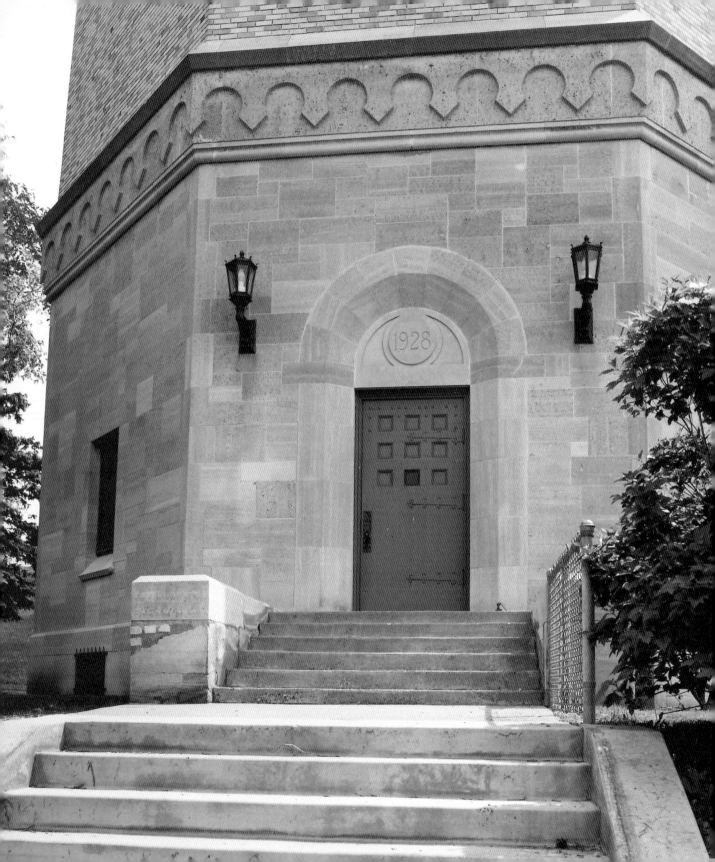

Native Kasota stone graces the Highland Park Water Tower.

Don Wong, 2000

Wigington turned to the Colonial Revival style for the homey Keller Golf Course clubhouse, built 1929.

Minnesota Historical Society

For the tower's building materials, Wigington chose a combination unique in his career: an unusual light-colored brick toned to match the cream Kasota stone trim. In his written recollections of his years in the City Architect's Office, Wigington was particularly proud of the Highland Park Water Tower, often quoting some unnamed source declaring it "the most beautiful water tower in the country." Because the tower was a unique project with a simple function, it is quite possible that it was a Wigington creation from top to bottom. In 1976 it became the first city project to be publicly recognized as the work of anyone but the City Architect himself.[1]

For Wigington's final park project of the 1920s, the Keller Golf Course clubhouse, he opted for a free variation of the Colonial Revival style. He was certainly not the first to make such a choice; architects had frequently employed the style to suggest an environment of privilege for the wealthy patrons who dominated the sport. Wigington's rendering of the style, however, is devoid of elitist resonances; the simple front elevation of the building suggests nothing more nor less than the shelter and coziness of a home at the end of the course.

Chelsea Heights
School, built 1932,
with its geometric
Moderne decoration,
still shows
Collegiate Gothic
influences in its
towering entry and
corner piers.

Don Wong, 2000

With the arrival of Charles Bassford in 1930, the City Architect's Office entered a new phase. Wigington was declared in charge of the drafting room just as the historical revival styles that had dominated American architectural practice for a century were finally laid to rest. Hereafter, all but additions to existing buildings would have to show credentials not of historical scholarship but of modern invention and utility. Once again, both the staff of the City Architect's Office and the City Architect himself had to learn a new vocabulary.

To most architects of the period, modern architecture did not mean the walls of concrete, steel, and glass that would soon co-opt the term "modernism." Rather, it meant the geometrical treatment of composition and

ornament that today we place under the rubric of Moderne or Art Deco. The City Architect's Office was among the earliest of St. Paul's architectural firms to adopt this fashion for major building design.

First off the drawing boards was Horace Mann Elementary School in 1930, with Carl H. Buetow, not Wigington, as architect in charge. Two years later Wigington applied his own version of Moderne decoration to a nearly identical plan at Chelsea Heights. His treatment of the building surface is remarkable for its underlying adherence to a Collegiate Gothic scheme, with towering entry bay, linear ornament, and massive corner piers still the dominant design features.[2]

The renovation and expansion of the St. Paul auditorium building offered Wigington his first full-fledged opportunity at Moderne design. For the auditorium façades he broke free from historical precedent altogether, creating sheer brick walls interrupted only by great vertical banks of windows and a geometrical frieze on the Kellogg Street side. The size of the Kellogg and Fifth street façades and the necessity of placing the entry bays at either end prevented Wigington from making his signature set piece in the center, unless the vast bay of windows is interpreted that way. Public reception of the building focused on its utility rather than its appearance; one reviewer remarked that the city now had "not an ornate memorial edifice" or "a gorgeous and imposing structure to point out to visiting strangers" but a "workable building." Wigington may have relished that description.[3]

For the remainder of the Depression years, much of the energy of the Bureau of Parks, Playgrounds, and Public Buildings was focused on expanding and rebuilding playground shelter houses. Wigington was project architect for all of them. Built over a seven-year period, the park shelters moved through three distinct design phases: Craftsman cottage, WPA rustic, and WPA Moderne. Shelter houses at Edgcumbe, Scheffer, St. Clair, Hazel Park, Belvidere, Sylvan, and Dayton's Bluff playgrounds, all built in 1934–35, were designed in the first vein. They continued to trade on the earlier association of park buildings with a kind of pastoral tranquillity. Largely of frame construction with stucco veneer and

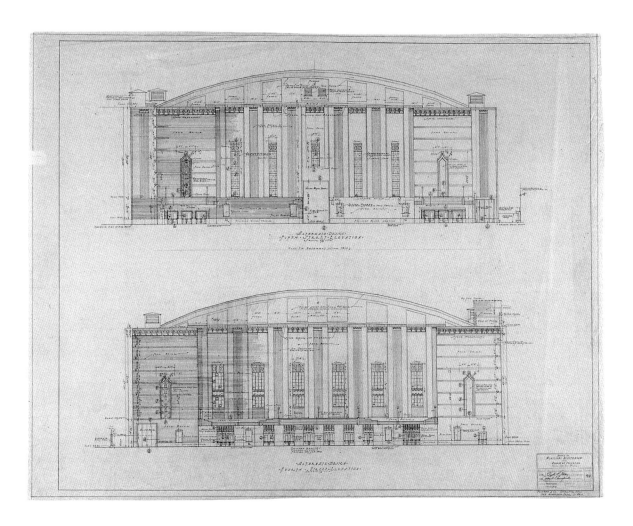

exposed rafter ends, they recalled English cottages or miniature manor houses. Already old-fashioned for their day, they were probably economically expedient during a time of little available funding. All have long since disappeared.

In 1936, with the Works Progress Administration at full tilt, Wigington developed a much more modern prototype for playground buildings

A vertical stone frieze punctuates the massive brick façade of the Roy Wilkins Auditorium.

Don Wong, 2000

planned under WPA auspices. Labeled "Typical Stone Shelter" on the working drawings, it featured rock-faced local limestone construction, simple squarish openings, and a central entry capped by a gable. Highland Park, West Minnehaha, and Baker playgrounds soon sported shelter houses of this rustic character. Because the terrain at Highland and Baker falls steeply away from the street, the basement level is fully exposed at the rear of each building, creating a sense of two quite different structures at front and rear. Each contained a large recreation room, hobby shops, and a basement room for "less violent games," in the words of the Baker playground center dedication announcement. Both of these buildings survive, though the Highland Park recreation building is closed, awaiting rediscovery.[4]

Rock-faced limestone gives the two-story Baker Playground Stone Shelter, built 1938, its rustic look.

Don Wong, 2000

The final stage in the evolution of the playground shelters occurred in the late 1930s, this time with WPA funding of city projects at its maximum level. The Hamline Playground Stone Shelter and Wilder Playground Building are both Moderne in sensibility, with faces of smooth-cut Mankato stone, a rectilinear geometry, and just enough subtle modeling of the wall surfaces to serve as ornament. They remain splendid examples of a monumental style shrunk to neighborhood scale.

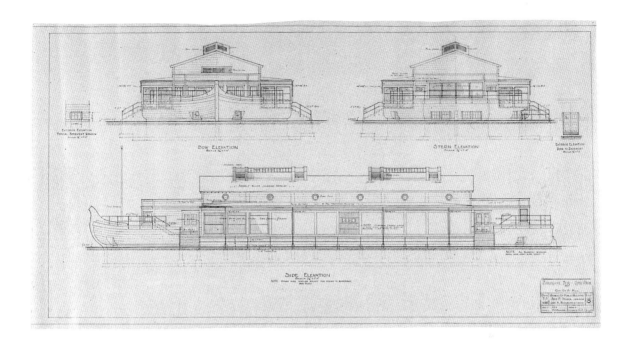

The largest park project to engage Wigington during the Depression was an animal house for Como Park. Wigington's initial conception—credited to Bassford in the press—was in the form of a 150-foot, wood-clad houseboat. Romantically dubbed Noah's Ark, it was to contain twenty-two cages, a monkey house, and a refectory, as well as a basement kitchen to provide food for both human and animal consumption. Its price tag was estimated to be $80,000. For reasons unknown, this concept died on the drawing board and a simpler Moderne structure went up in its place. Perhaps a frown from WPA officials was enough to squelch the romance of constructing in wood a building that so patently required the durability and low maintenance of masonry.[5]

What ultimately arose in the new zoo was a cluster of animal enclosures with a utilitarian central building, a stone barn for hoofed animals, a row of bear dens, and a monkey island. Because the original working drawings either have disappeared or fail to carry the initials of a project

Zoological Building, Como Park, 1935. Bow, stern, and side elevations (ink on linen, 22″ x 47″; collection of the City of St. Paul, Department of Technology and Management Services)

Proposed Pavilion for Harriet Island, 1940 (ink on paper
board, 15″ x 28″; Wigington Papers, Northwest Architectural
Archives, University of Minnesota Libraries)

architect, the designer of all of these structures is unknown. It is tempting to assign the main building to Wigington on the strength of an early presentation drawing that bears his initials. But as the best draftsman in the office, he would likely have been assigned that responsibility, whoever drafted the plans. The Moderne design for the main building was estimated to cost $60,000, a significant savings over the ark version; however, the final construction cost ultimately rose to $160,000, most of the tab picked up by the WPA.[6]

Wigington's climactic design among the host of park buildings and structures erected between the world wars was a new pavilion for Harriet Island, designed in 1938–40 and constructed in 1941. Its initial design placed it in the same Moderne vein as the Hamline and Wilder playground buildings. But over the course of long delays in funding, it took on an increasingly quiet, classical tone. The final design holds in perfect tension the formative moments of Wigington's career and his mature design sensibility. In that park structure he was able for the first time to combine his old love of picturesque skylines and arcades with a modernist's sense of planarity and frank utilitarianism. It is more than fitting that the building on Harriet Island should now be called the Wigington Pavilion.

Of all his designs for the City of St. Paul, Wigington expressed the deepest pride in his ice palaces. That may appear to be a strange choice, for each was doomed to a short life from the day of its creation, and none could capture anything but the most abbreviated range of an architect's skills. But they were as monumental in effect as anything built in the city, and like the Highland tower, each was entirely his. Over a span of ten years, from 1937 to 1947, he designed six ice castles and a number of secondary structures. Each was a Moderne shell with multiple references to the English Gothicism of his work thirty years earlier.

Perhaps better than any other buildings, Wigington's ice palaces captured the duality of his architectural outlook. Though largely spent in a single office, his career worked through a succession of building types and styles, and he was an office leader in understanding and embracing each new possibility of expression. But his most successful work also

The 1937 St. Paul Winter Carnival ice palace on the grounds of the State Capital. *Right:* under construction, January 27; *below:* during the festivities. *Facing page, top:* demolition with explosives; *bottom:* after the thaw.

Minnesota Historical Society

A pair of thrones await the St. Paul Winter Carnival royalty
at the 1940 ice palace in Como Park.

Minnesota Historical Society

looked back to history for inspiration—to both the history of architecture itself and his own personal history as a fledgling designer under the tutelage of Thomas Kimball. The sheer walls and zigzag contours of his ice palaces were paeans to modernism as Wigington understood it. But the walls met the sky with a dancing line, and the rhythm of the dance jumped from surface to surface on their undulating sides. This was Gothicism as Wigington practiced it—not a recapturing of something ancient or arcane but an exuberant elaboration of the everyday.

ARCHITECTURAL LEGACY

Wigington in his seventies

Carolyn Pemberton

5

WHO WILL SPEAK FOR ME

Herein lie buried many things which if read with patience may show the strange meanings of being black here at the dawning of the Twentieth Century. The meaning is not without interest to you, Gentle Reader; for the problem of the Twentieth Century is the problem of the color-line . . . . Leaving, then, the white world, I have stepped within the Veil, raising it that you may view faintly its deeper recesses . . . . [N]eed I add that I who speak here am bone of the bone and flesh of them that live within the Veil?

W. E. B. Du Bois, *The Souls of Black Folk*

CLARENCE WIGINGTON's copy of *The Souls of Black Folk* is autographed, "Very sincerely yours, W. E. B. Du Bois, Atlanta, Ga., November 9, 1909." The volume is also filled with comments jotted by Wigington as he read and reread this seminal treatise on black America. In one famous passage, Du Bois describes how "this American world . . . yields [to the Negro] no true self-consciousness, but only lets him see himself through the revelation of the other world. It is a peculiar sensation, this double consciousness, this sense of always looking at one's self by the tape of a world that looks on in amused contempt and pity. One ever feels his two-ness, an American, a Negro." In the margin next to this text, Wigington wrote, "How true." Where Du Bois comments on how the American Negro "simply wishes to make it possible for a man to be both a Negro and an American, without being cursed and spit upon by his fellows," Wigington wrote, "This simple ambition is slowly but surely lifting the colored American into the ranks of achievement all along the line."[1]

Wigington was proud of his own professional achievements. He also understood the uniqueness of his position. From humble beginnings, he had risen to a place of prominence in a civil service system slow to hire black employees. With a combination of talent, diplomacy, and political sagacity, he held that place through the tenure of four City Architects over a span of 27 years. Embracing the obligations and leadership responsibilities of his position of privilege, he used it as a conduit for employment opportunities for others.

In nineteenth-century parlance, Wigington was considered a "race man." He clearly identified himself with the interests of the African American community. He spoke and wrote on behalf of those who were politically and economically disenfranchised. In his quiet and conservative way, he provided effective leadership by the only means known to him—brokering concessions through the agency of powerful and influential whites. In his later years, protestation and agitation—increasingly the weapons of choice of younger, more aggressive leaders—were not options for him. He preferred the civility of debate and moral suasion. Toward the end of his life, Wigington expressed frustration with the indignities still experienced by African Americans. Although he preferred diplomacy to civil disobedience, he empathized with the impatience of the younger generation, perhaps recognizing that many in his generation, too, criticized Booker T. Washington's "gradualism" in their struggle for the rights of citizenship.

These two aspects of Wigington's life—his architectural career and his work as a civic leader—shape the major questions in evaluating the significance of his achievements. What does his life story tell us about the struggle for direction and meaning experienced by his generation of African Americans? How does his career inform us about the nature of race relations in the Twin Cities during the first half of the twentieth century?

Many of Wigington's generation, born after the end of the Civil War, possessed a thirst for education and a strong work ethic. What they lacked were opportunities for self-improvement. A fortunate few found their way into newly established educational institutions for recently freed men and women. Others acquired trade skills through apprenticeships provided by well-intentioned whites. Unfortunately, the masses of African Americans—former slaves, the newly freed, the next generation—were left to find their destinies without benefit of education or training.

The nature of race relations at the turn of the century suggests a degree of paternalism expressed by influential whites towards blacks, especially those showing promise. Given the prevailing stereotypes popular in the culture, black people with intellectual vigor and artistic talent were considered anomalies. However, as persons of refinement, they were deemed closer in social stature to upper-class whites than lower-class whites. White philanthropy was directed at cultivating these refined traits for the purpose of general racial uplift and peaceful race relations. Therefore, it was not unusual for black youths of promise to be placed under the tutorship or mentorship of skilled or professional white people.

Young Wigington was surely the beneficiary of such white altruism. There seems to be no compelling reason, other than the recommendation of Thomas Kimball's secretary, for Kimball to have offered him an apprenticeship. Kimball did not seek him out. Perhaps, given the paucity of trained black professionals in the field of architecture, there was something to be gained by the novelty of having a black apprentice.

At the turn of the century, in Minnesota and elsewhere, African Americans were not well represented in any of the skilled trades. Very often, but not always, trade guilds and unions excluded blacks from apprenticeships; white skilled laborers were preferred.[2] Most blacks, men and women, were relegated to undesirable or low-wage jobs in the service sectors of the economy. However, educated black professionals—businessmen, doctors, lawyers—were highly respected and patronized by whites. In St. Paul, businessman T. H. Lyles, attorney Frederick L. McGhee, and Doctors R. S. Brown, Sr., and Val Do Turner, among others, all had mixed clientele.

When he moved to Minnesota, Wigington was adopted into that community of black professionals. These men validated the philosophies espoused by both Washington and Du Bois concerning the ultimate road to achievement and success for black Americans. Their training placed them squarely within the ranks of Du Bois's Talented Tenth. And their business sense, work ethic, and ability to understand whites and the politics of race reflected Washington's sensibilities. Yet, unlike Washington, they seem to have been able to further their agenda without either alienating whites or compromising their own positions on civil rights. They were quintessential diplomats, moving comfortably between two socially separate but mutually dependent communities. Though it was Wigington's work as an architect that sustained him, the affirmation he received from the black community and the leadership opportunities it provided him may have nurtured him through the difficult times in his personal and professional life.

Among the factors threatening the security of his position with the City of St. Paul were the vagaries of the economy, the internal politics of the City Architect's Office, and the personalities and political fortunes of the City Architects to whom he reported. After resigning when City Architect Charles Hausler was removed from office, Wigington may have learned that to guarantee employment in City Hall one had to eschew politics. Because his skills and versatility had made him a key member of his department, he was soon brought back on board.

As senior architectural draftsman, privy to all operational aspects of the office, Wigington was equally knowledgeable about design, structural engineering, construction materials, and stylistic options. His skills as a team leader, too, made him an ideal candidate for advancement. So there is little to explain why he seems never to have aspired to the position of City Architect. The most probable scenario is that Wigington, well in tune with his times, realized that, as a black man—ambition and talent notwithstanding—he would never be appointed City Architect. Judging from existing records, all appointments to that position came from outside the office and generally went to architects with well-established private practices. So in spite of his friendships with city officials, his involvement in the Republican Party, and his working relationships with three Minnesota governors, Wigington, a long-time civil servant, was unlikely to attain the office. He poured his energies instead into his extraordinary work with the Urban League.

Wigington seemed not to be worrying about missed opportunities when he wrote of his life in St. Paul:

> Each night, year after year, I thanked Almighty God for granting me some degree of ability, a stout heart of courage, a mind of sincere understanding, a sound and liberal appreciation of my good neighbors, a hope and trust that man's inhumanity to man in some areas of my country would stop NOW, not next year, not a generation from now, but NOW.[3]

Within the context of American social history, Clarence Wigington's race and origins may be as important as his professional achievements in the mark he left on St. Paul. He struggled, as Du Bois put it, "to merge his double self into a better and truer self." St. Paulites of all races enjoy a richer landscape because of his architectural work. And his impact as an African American leader—as a role model, as one able to move the white bureaucracy, as a person who lived his convictions and found the energy to make a difference in his community—cannot be calculated. He left his city stronger because of these efforts, and his legacy of hard work and service is a model for all.

Samples of Wigington's Work in St. Paul

1. Baker Playground Stone Shelter, 209 West Page Street
2. Chelsea Heights Elementary School, 1557 Huron Street
3. Clarence W. Wigington Pavilion (Harriet Island Park Stone Pavilion), Harriet Island
4. Cleveland Junior High School, 1000 Walsh Street
   Edgcumbe Elementary School, see Talmud Torah Academy
5. Fire Station #10, 750 Randolph Avenue
6. Fire Station #17, 1226 Payne Avenue
7. Fire Station #5, 860 Ashland Avenue
8. Hamline Playground Stone Shelter, 1570 Lafond Avenue
   Harriet Island Park Stone Pavilion, see Clarence W. Wigington Pavilion
9. Highland Park Water Tower, Snelling Avenue at Ford Parkway
10. Holman Airfield Administration Building, east end of St. Lawrence
11. Homecroft Elementary School, 1845 Sheridan Avenue
12. Ice Palace, State Capitol, 1937
13. Ice Palaces, Como Park, 1940, 1941
14. Keller Golf Course Clubhouse, 2166 Maplewood Drive
15. Mann Elementary School, East Addition, 2001 Edgcumbe
    Marshall Junior High School, see Webster Magnet Elementary School
16. Monroe Junior High School, 810 Palace Avenue
17. Private Residence, 1592 Western Avenue North
18. Private Residence, 1988 West Princeton
19. Private Residence, 2210 Edgcumbe Road
20. Private Residence, 357 Woodlawn Avenue
21. Roy Wilkins Auditorium Building Façade, West 5th Street west of Rice Park
22. Talmud Torah Academy (Edgcumbe Elementary School), 1287 Ford Parkway
    Unidale Playground Building, see West Minnehaha Playground Building
23. Washington High School, 1041 Marion Street
24. Webster Magnet Elementary School, West Building (Marshall Junior High School), 62 North Grotto Street
25. West Minnehaha (Unidale) Playground Building, 685 West Minnehaha Avenue
26. Wilder Playground Building, 958 Jessie Street
27. Wilson Junior High School, 631 North Albert Street

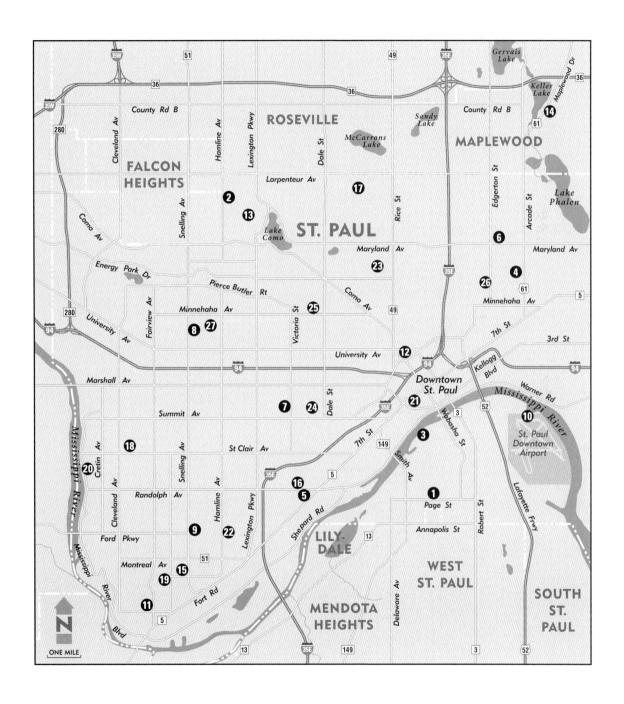

APPENDIX
WIGINGTON'S BUILDINGS

This list of the works of Clarence Wigington consists of three parts:

    A. St. Paul buildings on which Wigington was the architect in charge;

    B. St. Paul buildings on which Wigington was a draftsman;

    C. Wigington's independent commissions.

Buildings that appear in boldface are extant, and some minor remodelings may also survive. Addresses are taken from city directories current at time of construction and may not be consistent with modern addresses.

The information in this list is drawn from highly varied sources, which are included after the construction dates for the convenience of subsequent researchers. The most authoritative sources for attributions and design dates are the working drawings, which after 1923 usually carried the initials of draftsmen and the "architect in charge." As construction documents for numerous projects could not be located, and many drawings carry no initials in the "architect in charge" box, we can safely assume that many of Wigington's designs remain anonymous or have been attributed to the city architect. Several buildings that are frequently attributed to Wigington, either speculatively or on the basis of documents now lost or misplaced, appear in section B marked with an asterisk; I was unable to confirm the attributions.

Building permits (available at the Department of Licensing and Environmental Protection, City of St. Paul) and newspaper notices of building dedications (located in the microfiche news clipping files at the St. Paul Public Library) are here accepted as authoritative for dates of initiation and completion of construction. However, many park and playground buildings were constructed without permits or public fanfare. An attempt has been made to fill in these dates (indicated by brackets) on the basis of city construction scheduling common to buildings of that type. A question mark indicates uncertainty about whether the project was built.

Other information was garnered from Jene T. Sigvertsen, *An Inventory of Saint Paul Public School Facilities from the Past to the Present* (St. Paul Public Schools, 1994). The Northwest Architectural Archives holds lists of drawings that were assembled from the files at the City Architect's Office and the offices of the St. Paul Public School District; these are cited below as "Lists of Drawings, NWAA." Unless otherwise noted, the Wigington correspondence and records cited below are in the Wigington/Pemberton Family Papers at the NWAA.

Paul Clifford Larson

Abbreviations:

SPCH – Real Estate Office, St. Paul City Hall
SPSD – Facilities Management Office, St. Paul Public School District
MHS – Ramsey County Archives, Minnesota Historical Society Library
NWAA – Northwest Architectural Archives, University of Minnesota

A. St. Paul City Projects, C. W. Wigington, Lead Architect

Homecroft Elementary School, 1845 Sheridan Avenue
  Designed 1918–20, built 1921. *Appeal,* Mar. 16, 1918; *Improvement Bulletin,* Jan. 11, 1919, May 10, 1919; unsigned drawings at SPCH.
Battle Creek Park Log Shelter, 1851 North Point Douglas Road
  Designed 1923–26, built 1923–26. Rendering and drawings at SPCH: CWW as draftsman; no one listed in charge.
Van Buren Elementary School remodeling, 275 Maple Avenue
  Designed 1924, built 1924. Drawings not found; CWW cited as architect in charge in Lists of Drawings, NWAA.
Wilson Junior High School, 631 North Albert Street
  Designed 1924, built 1924–25. Drawings at SPSD: WMG, CWW, LDM, WRW, HAM as draftsmen; no one listed in charge; cited as Wigington design at time of his retirement.
Marshall Junior High School (Webster Magnet Elementary), 62 North Grotto Street
  Designed 1924, built 1924–25. Drawings at SPSD: WMG, TJM, HAM, LDM, WRW, LCB as draftsmen; no one listed in charge; based on Wilson plan and executed six months later; cited as Wigington design at time of his retirement.

Cleveland Junior High School, 1000 Walsh Street

Designed 1924, built 1925. Drawings for primary construction not found; detailing very similar to Wilson.

Monroe Junior High School, 810 Palace Avenue

Designed 1924, built 1925–26. Drawings at SPSD: LDM, WMG, HW, TJM, HPS, Boyer, CWW, Minuti as draftsmen; CWW in charge of exterior design.

Washington High School, 1041 Marion Street

Designed 1924, built 1926. Drawings at SPSD: WMG, RCP, TJM, LCB, JAS, LDM, CWW, HWC as draftsmen; CWW in charge.

Highland Park Flagstaff a.id Monument, Highland Golf Course

Designed 1926, built 1926. Drawings at SPCH: CWW as draftsman; no one listed in charge.

Langford Park Warming House, Langford Park Place near Knapp Street

Designed 1926, built 1926. Drawings at SPCH: CWW as draftsman and in charge.

Highland Park Water Tower, Snelling Avenue at Ford Parkway

Designed 1928, built 1928. Drawings at SPCH: CWW as main draftsman; CWW in charge.

Adams School regrading, 615 South Chatsworth Street

Designed 1928, built 1928. Drawings at SPSD: CWW as draftsman; no one listed in charge.

Ramsey County School for Boys, Highwood Avenue

Designed 1928, built 1928. Drawings not found; CWW cited as architect in charge in Lists of Drawings, NWAA.

Battle Creek Park Picnic Shelter, 1851 North Point Douglas Road

Designed 1929, built 1929. Drawings at SPCH: CWW and CHB as draftsmen; no one listed in charge.

Fire Station #17, 1226 Payne Avenue

Designed 1929, built 1929. Drawings at SPCH: CWW in charge.

Keller Golf Course Clubhouse, 2166 Maplewood Drive

Designed 1929, built 1929. Drawings at SPCH: ES, FSK, CHB, CWW as draftsmen; CWW in charge.

Fire Station #5, 860 Ashland Avenue

Designed 1929, built 1930. Drawings at SPCH: CWW in charge.

Roy Wilkins Auditorium Building Façade, West 5th Street west of Rice Park

Designed 1929–31, built 1929–31. Drawings at SPCH: CWW drawing of main elevation; attribution of exterior design from many sources.

Arlington Playground Building remodeling, 665 Rose Avenue East
Designed 1931, built 1931. Drawings at SPCH: CWW as draftsman; no one listed in charge.

Chelsea Heights Elementary School, 1557 Huron Street
Designed 1932, built 1932. Drawings at SPSD: elevations CWW, plans and sections WMG; no one listed in charge.

Catherine Welsh Smith Memorial, Rice Street
Designed 1932, built [1932]. Drawings at SPCH: CWW as draftsman and in charge.

Veterans Hospital addition, Fort Snelling
Designed 1932, built [1933]. Drawings not found; CWW cited as architect in charge in Lists of Drawings, NWAA.

Phalen Park Refectory remodeling, West Phalen Drive
Designed 1933, built 1933. Drawings at SPCH: CWW as draftsman; no one listed in charge.

Como Park Barn, Como Park Maintenance Area
Designed 1934, built [1934]. Drawings at SPCH: AL, CHS, MAW, HAM as draftsmen; CWW in charge.

Holman Airfield Airplane Hangar addition, east end of St. Lawrence
Designed 1934, built [1934]. Drawings at SPCH: CWW and LSJ as draftsmen; CWW in charge.

Scheffer Playground Shelter, 224 Lafond Avenue
Designed 1934, built 1935. Drawings at SPCH: FWC as draftsman; CWW in charge.

Rice and Lawson Playground Shelter, 1025 Rice Street
Designed 1934, built 1935. Drawings at SPCH: PJL, FWC as draftsman; CWW in charge.

Hazel Park Playground Shelter, 952 Hazel Street
Designed 1934, built 1935. Drawings at SPCH: CWW, Ash, Donohue as draftsmen; CWW in charge.

St. Clair Playground Shelter House, 265 Oneida Street
Designed 1934, built 1935. Drawings at SPCH: CWA #2804; CWW in charge.

Edgcumbe Playground Shelter House, 320 South Griggs Street
Designed 1934, built [1935]. Drawings at SPCH: CWW in charge.

South St. Anthony Playground Shelter House, 890 Cromwell
Designed 1934, built [1935]. Drawings at SPCH: RER as draftsman; CWW in charge.

Unidale Playground Building addition, 721 West Minnehaha Avenue
Designed 1934, built [1935]. Drawings at SPCH: FWC as draftsman; CWW in charge.

Tourist Information Building, Robert Street and Kellogg Boulevard
Designed 1934, built [1935]. Drawings at SCCH: CWW as draftsman; no one listed in charge.

Como Park Lakeside Pavilion restoration, 1360 North Lexington Avenue
Drafted 1934–35, built ?. Drawings at SPCH: CWW in charge.

Phalen Park Bath House repairs, 1350 Earl Street
Designed 1935, built [1935]. Drawings at SPCH: CWW in charge.

Highland Park Swimming Pool revisions to drawings, 1840 Edgcumbe Road
Designed 1935, built [1935]. Drawings at SPCH: RER and HAM as draftsmen; CWW in charge.

Belvidere Playground Shelter House, 301 East Belvidere Street
Designed 1935, built 1936. Drawings at SPCH: FWC and CWW as draftsmen; CWW in charge.

Sylvan Playground Shelter House, 77 West Rose Avenue
Designed 1935, built [1936]. Drawings at SPCH: WWJ and FLH as draftsmen; CWW in charge.

Aldine Playground Building remodeling, 1717 Iglehart Avenue
Designed 1935, built [1936]. Drawings at SPCH: FLH and PJL as draftsmen; CWW in charge.

Dayton's Bluff (Mound's Park) Playground Shelter House, Euclid Street at Hudson Road
Designed 1935, built [1936]. Drawings at SPCH: RER as draftsman; CWW in charge.

Scheffer Elementary School remodeling, 237 Thomas Avenue
Designed 1935, built [1936]. Drawings at MHS: WWJ as draftsman; CWW in charge.

Highland Park Stone Shelter, Montreal Avenue at Hamline Avenue
Designed c. 1935, built 1936. Drawings not found; similar to Baker Playground Stone Shelter.

Como Park Zoo Building in the form of an ark, Como Park Zoo
Designed 1935, not built. Drawings at SPCH: CWW draftsman and in charge (built to different plans in 1936).

Como Park Golf Course Clubhouse remodelings, 1431 North Lexington Parkway
Designed 1935–39, built [1936–40]. Drawings at SPCH: CWW in charge.

Phalen Park Boat Dock and Canoe Racks, West Phalen Drive
Designed 1936, built [1936]. Drawings at SPCH: CWW as draftsman; no one listed in charge.

Cleveland Junior High School addition and remodeling, 1000 Walsh Street
Designed 1936, built 1937. Drawings at SPSD: WMG, CHS, TJM, EVS, HAM, RFH as draftsmen; CWW in charge.

Edgcumbe Playground Shelter House addition, 320 South Griggs Street
Designed 1936, built [1937]. Drawings at SPCH: CWW as draftsman; no one listed in charge.

Edgcumbe Playground Building addition, 320 South Griggs Street
Designed 1936, built [1937]. Drawings at SPCH: CWW in charge.

Ice Palace, State Capitol Mall
Designed 1936–37, built 1937. Drawings at SPCH: CWW as draftsman.

Cedar Streeet Toboggan Slide, Cedar Street below the capitol
Designed 1936–37, built 1937. Drawings at SPCH: CWW as draftsman.

Mounds Park Toboggan Slide, Burns Avenue south of Griffith Street
Designed 1937, built 1937. Drawings at SPCH: HAM as draftsman; CWW in charge.

Unidale (West Minnehaha) Playground Building, 685 West Minnehaha Avenue
Designed 1937–38, built 1940. Drawings at SPCH: EWO, CWW, HAM as draftsmen; CWW in charge.

Ice Palace, Rice Park
Designed 1937–38, not built. Drawings at SPCH: CWW in charge of this design, but built to plans of others.

Como Park Zoo Refectory Stand, Como Park Zoo
Designed 1938, built [1938]. Drawings at SPCH: HAM as draftsman; CWW in charge.

Como Park Conservatory addition, Como Park
Designed 1938, built 1939. Drawings not found; CWW cited as architect in charge in Lists of Drawings, NWAA.

Monroe Junior High School Auditorium, Clifton Street south of Palace Avenue
Designed 1938, built 1939. Drawings at SPSD: GHS, RPP, WMG, GMM, CWW, JL, WRW as draftsmen: CWW in charge.

Baker Playground Stone Shelter, 209 West Page Street
Designed 1938, built 1939. Drawings at SPCH: JEL as draftsman; CWW in charge.

Edgcumbe Elementary School (Talmud Torah Academy), 1287 Ford Parkway
Designed 1938, built 1939. Drawings at successor school, Talmud Torah: CWW in charge.

Harding High School addition, 516 Earl Street
Designed 1938, built [1939]. Drawings at SPSD: Miller, Witte, CWW as draftsmen; CWW in charge.

Hamline Playground Stone Shelter, 1570 Lafond Avenue
  Designed 1938, built 1940. Drawings at SPCH: CWW as main draftsman and in charge.

Holman Airfield Administration Building, East end of St. Lawrence
  Designed 1938–41, built 1938–41. Drawings at SPCH: WMG, PVU, HAM as draftsmen; CWW in charge.

Chelsea Heights Elementary School addition, Hoyt Avenue and Chelsea Street
  Designed 1939, built 1939. Drawings at SPSD: Witte, JES, Donohue, EWO as draftsmen; CWW in charge.

Mann Elementary School, east addition, 2001 West Eleanor Avenue
  Designed 1939, built 1939. Drawings at SPSD: WRW, GMM, Donohue as draftsmen; CWW in charge.

Como Park Hoofed Animal House drawing revisions, Como Park Zoo
  Designed 1939, built [1939]. Drawings at SPCH: revised drawings by CWW; no one listed in charge.

Como Park Picnic Pavilion, Buelah Lane
  Designed 1939, built [1939]. Drawings at SPCH: WMG as draftsman; CWW in charge.

Murray Junior High School addition, 1450 South Grantham Street
  Designed 1939, built ?. Drawings at SPSD: WMG as draftsman; CWW in charge.

Ice Palace, Como Park
  Designed 1939–40, built 1940. Drawings at SPCH: CWW sole draftsman and architect in charge.

Fire King's Throne, Wabasha Street near 4th Street
  Designed 1939–40, built 1940. Drawings at SPCH: CWW sole draftsman and architect in charge.

Harriet Island Park Stone Pavilion (Clarence W. Wigington Pavilion), Harriet Island
  Designed 1939–40, built 1941. Drawings at SPCH: CWW in charge.

Fire Station #10, 750 Randolph Avenue
  Designed 1940, built 1940. Drawings at SPCH: CWW in charge.

Phalen Park Canoe Racks addition, West Phalen Drive
  Designed 1940, built [1940]. Drawings at SPCH: CWW as draftsman and in charge.

Phalen Park Bandstand addition, West Phalen Drive
  Designed 1940, built [1940]. Drawings at SPCH: CWW as draftsman and in charge.

Como Park Barn addition, Como Park Maintenance Area
  Designed 1940, built [1940]. Drawings at SPCH: WGM as draftsman; CWW in charge.

Highland Park Toboggan Slide, Highland Park
  Designed 1940, built [1940]. Drawings at SPCH: RPP as draftsman; CWW in charge.
Fire Station #22 remodeling, 291 Front Avenue
  Designed 1940, built ?. Drawings not found; attributed to CWW in notes at NWAA; no permit.
Wilder Playground Building, 958 Jessie Street
  Designed 1940–41, built 1941. Drawings at SPCH: CWW as main draftsman and in charge.
Ice Palace, Como Park
  Designed 1940–41, built 1941. Drawings at SPCH: CWW sole draftsman and architect in charge.
Highland Park Caddy House, Highland Golf Course
  Designed 1941, built 1941. Drawings at SPCH: CWW in charge.
Mounds Park Drinking Fountain, Mounds Boulevard west of Earl Street
  Designed 1941, built [1941]. Drawings at SPCH: CWW as main draftsman and in charge.
Neill Elementary School remodeling, 325 Laurel Avenue
  Designed 1941, built [1941]. Drawings at MHS: CWW in charge.
Groveland Park Elementary School library remodeling, 2045 St. Clair Avenue
  Designed 1941, built [1941]. Drawing at SPSD: CWW as draftsman and in charge.
Ice Palace, Highland Park
  Designed 1941–42, built 1942. Drawings at SPCH: CWW in charge (not completed).
Ramsey Playground Community Building remodeling, Ramsey Street at Smith Avenue
  Designed 1941–42, built [1942]. Drawings at SPCH: CWW in charge.
Hamline Playground Sandbox Shelter, 1570 Lafond Avenue
  Designed 1942, built ?. Drawings at SPCH: CWW draftsman and in charge (not built?).
Phalen Park Golf Course Sheltered Bench, Phalen Park Golf Course
  Designed 1943, built [1943]. Drawings at SPCH: CWW as draftsman; no one listed in charge.
Phalen Park Pavilion remodeling, West Phalen Drive
  Designed 1944, built [1944]. Drawings at SPCH: WMG as draftsman; CWW in charge.

Phalen Park Pavilion lunch counter, West Phalen Drive
Designed 1946, built [1946]. Drawings at SPCH: CWW as draftsman and in charge.

Belvidere Playground Emergency Housing, 301 East Belvidere Street
Designed 1946, built [1946]. Drawings at SPCH: CWW in charge.

Ice Palace, Highland Park
Designed 1946–47, unfinished. Drawings at SPCH: CWW as draftsman; work completed by others.

Phalen Park Pavilion sink cabinet, West Phalen Drive
Designed 1947, built [1947]. Drawings at SPCH: CWW as draftsman and in charge.

Como Park Greenhouse smokestack, Como Park
Designed 1947, built [1947]. Drawings at SPCH: drawings by WGM; CWW in charge.

Highland Park Comfort Station, Montreal Avenue west of Hamline Avenue
Designed 1947, built [1947]. Drawings at SPCH: drawings by CWW; CWW in charge.

Phalen Park Boat Dock addition, West Phalen Drive
Designed 1947, built [1947]. Drawings at SPCH: drawings by CWW; no one listed in charge.

Phalen Park Diving Platform, 1350 Earl Street
Designed 1948, built [1948]. Drawings at SPCH: drawings by Christen; CWW in charge.

B. City Projects, C. W. Wigington, Draftsman

McClellan (Como Park) Elementary School, 780 West Wheelock Parkway
Designed 1915–16, built 1916–17. *Improvement Bulletin,* June 26, 1915; rendering *Improvement Bulletin,* July 24, 1915, Nov. 27, 1915, Jan. 29, 1916; drawings at SPSD: "by Wigington" added in corner of drawing of main elevation.

Phalen Park Shelter, West Phalen Drive
Designed 1923, built 1923. Drawings at SPCH: CWW and JAS as draftsmen; no one listed in charge.

Harding High School, 516 Earl Street
Designed 1923–24, built 1926. Drawings at SPSD: TJM, CHB, LDM, HW, JAS, LCB, CWW, HPS, Witte as draftsmen; CHB in charge.

*Douglas Relief (Bryant) School,** 694 Charlton Street
Designed 1924, built 1925. Drawings at MHS: WMH, JAS, CWW, CHB, JAS, HPS as draftsmen; WMG in charge.

Johnson High School addition, 740 York Avenue
  Designed 1924, built 1925. Drawings at SPSD: LDM, TJM, WMG, CWW (interior trim details) as draftsmen; RLE in charge.
Hendricks School remodeling, 320 Midway Parkway
  Designed 1925, built 1925. Drawings at MHS: TJM, CWW (cornice and entry) as draftsmen; RLE in charge.
Crowley School remodeling, 82 East Delos Street
  Designed 1925, built 1925. Drawings at MHS: CWW as draftsman; RLE in charge.
*Macalaster (Ramsey) Junior High School, 25 Cambridge Street
  Designed 1926, built 1926–27. Drawings at SPSD: WMG, TJM, CWW (interior casework) as draftsmen; no one listed in charge.
Margaret Playground Gymnasium addition, 668 Earl Street
  Designed 1928, built 1929. Drawings at SPCH: HPS, CWW (one tracing) as draftsmen; no one listed in charge.
Highland Park Shelter House, Montreal Avenue west of Hamline Avenue
  Designed 1929, built 1929. Drawings at SPCH: checked by CWW; HAM in charge.
*St. Paul Public Safety Building, 101 East 10th Street
  Designed 1929–30, built 1930. Drawings at SPCH: CWW (column and door details) and others; no one listed in charge.
*Como Park Zoo Main Building, Como Park Zoo
  Designed 1935–36, built 1936. Drawings at SPCH: WMG and RER as draftsmen; no one listed in charge; published rendering by CWW.
Highland Park Bath House, 1840 Edgcumbe Road
  Designed 1936–37, built 1937. Drawings at SPCH: CWW and PFU as draftsmen; no one listed in charge.

C. Independent Projects, C. W. Wigington, Architect

Isaac Bailey House, 2816 Pratt Street, Omaha
  Designed 1908, built 1908. Building permit.
Potato chip factory, not located, Omaha
  Designed 1908, built 1908. "The Man of the Month: Clarence Wigington," *Eyes* 1 (May 1946); probably razed.
Sheridan County Courthouse and Jail, Sheridan, Wyo.
  Designed 1908, not built. "The Man of the Month," *Eyes* 1 (May 1946); built to other plans.

Broomfield and Crutchfield Duplex 1, 2502–04 Lake Street, Omaha
Designed 1909, built 1913. Building permit.
Broomfield and Crutchfield Duplex 2, 2508–10 Lake Street, Omaha
Designed 1909, built 1913. Building permit.
Administration building and two dormitories, National Religious Training School, Durham, N.C.
Designed 1910, built 1910. CWW application for registration as an architect in California, Feb. 23, 1950.
St. John's AME Church addition, 617 North 18th Street, Omaha
Designed 1910, built 1910–11. Building permit; destroyed by fire c. 1918.
Thomas P. Peterson House, 3908 North 18th Street, Omaha
Designed ?, built 1912. Building permit.
Leonard B. Britt House, 2519 Maple Street, Omaha
Designed ?, built 1912. Building permit.
Zion Baptist Church, 2215 Grant Street, Omaha
Designed 1910–13, built 1913–14. Building permit.
Hollis M. Johnson House, 1820 Lothrop Street, Omaha
Designed ?, built 1914. Building permit.
Flats, 1832–34, South 11th Street, Omaha
Designed ?, built 1914. Building permit.
Duplex, 125–27 South 38th Street, Omaha
Designed ?, built 1914. Building permit.
Catherine McVay House, 1988 West Princeton Avenue, St. Paul
Designed 1917, built 1917. Building permit.
Housing development for T. D. McAnulty (9 houses), not located, St. Paul
Designed c. 1917, built 1917–20. CWW application for registration as an architect in California.
Twin City Milk Producers Association Plant remodeling, Cedar, Minn.
Designed 1920, built 1920. Twin City Milk Producers 1920 Annual Report, CWW application for registration as an architect in California.
Twin City Milk Producers Association Plant, Jefferson Highway, Elk River, Minn.
Designed 1920, built 1920–21. Twin City Milk Producers 1920 Annual Report, CWW application for registration as an architect in California.
Twin City Milk Producers Association Plant, Northfield, Minn.
Designed 1920, built 1921. Twin City Milk Producers 1920 Annual Report, CWW application for registration as an architect in California.

Twin City Milk Producers Association Plant remodeling, Robbinsdale, Minn.
Designed 1920, built 1921. Twin City Milk Producers 1920 Annual Report, CWW application for registration as an architect in California.

St. James AME Church, 624 West Central Avenue, St. Paul
Designed 1922, partially built 1922–26. *Northwestern Bulletin,* Aug. 19, 1922; *St. Paul Echo,* Jan. 16, 1926; basement only; superstructure to different plans in 1948.

Pyramid Building, North Highland Place and Lyndale Avenue, Minneapolis
Designed 1923, not built. *Minneapolis Messenger,* June 9, 1923.

Gopher Lodge No. 105, BPOEW, Rondo Avenue near Mackubin Street, St. Paul
Designed 1925, not built. *Bulletin-Appeal,* Jan. 17, 1925.

Sons of Jacob Synagogue, 1466 Portland Avenue, St. Paul
Designed 1946–48, built 1946–48. Letter to McAnulty, Aug. 29, 1948, NWAA; building permit; plan only partly realized; building purchased and expanded by a Christian congregation.

St. George's Greek Orthodox Chapel, 1111 Summit Avenue?, St. Paul
Designed 1948, built ?. Letter to McAnulty, Aug. 29, 1948, NWAA.

Jack G. Butwin house, 357 Woodlawn Avenue, St. Paul
Designed 1948, built 1948. Letter to McAnulty, Aug. 29, 1948, NWAA.

Simon Klein house, 2110 Edgcumbe Road, St. Paul
Designed 1949, built 1950. CWW application for registration as an architect in California.

Highland Village site plan, Ford Parkway and Cleveland Avenue, St. Paul
Designed 1949, built ?. Letter to Welch, Draper and Kramer, Oct. 17, 1949.

Crescent Bay Masonic Lodge addition and alterations, 1720 Broadway Avenue, Santa Monica, Calif.
Designed 1950, built 1950. Letter to Paul Wigington, Sept. 25, 1950; rendering. Status unknown.

Fidelity Lodge No. 10, F & AM, 3007 Logan Avenue, San Diego, Calif.
Designed 1950, built 1950–51. Letter of agreement, Sept. 16, 1950; other correspondence; engineering calculations. Status unknown.

Roberson-Williams Office Building, Central Avenue and 41st Place, Los Angeles, Calif.
Designed 1950, not built. Client agreement, Sept. 16, 1950.

Macedonia Baptist Church addition and alterations, 1755 East 47th Street, Los Angeles, Calif.
Designed 1955, built 1956. Client agreement, July 1, 1955; drawing. Status unknown.

Greater Olivet Baptist Church addition and alterations, 1646 East 47th Street, Los Angeles, Calif.

Designed 1955, built ?. Contract, Oct. 2, 1955. Status unknown.

George Smith building addition and alterations, 2822–24 South Western Avenue, Los Angeles, Calif.

Designed 1955, not built. Contract, July 1, 1955.

Greater First Baptist Church addition and alterations, 7728 South Broadway Street, Los Angeles, Calif.

Designed 1957, built 1957. Specifications, working drawings. Status unknown.

James Griffin house, 1592 Western Avenue, St. Paul

Designed 1957, built 1957. James Griffin.

South Los Angeles Mortuary, 1020 West 94th Street, Los Angeles, Calif.

Designed 1957, built ?. Letter with preliminary drawings, Nov. 26, 1955. Status unknown.

Harvey A. Moss house and garage, not located, Minneapolis

Designed 1959, built ?. Letter to Moss, Aug. 12, 1959. Status unknown.

Masonic Temple, St. Paul

Designed 1959, not built. Working drawing.

AAA Club remodeling, 85–87 Kellogg Boulevard East, St. Paul

Designed 1962, built 1963. Letter to Mutual of Omaha, Jan. 29, 1966.

Sterling Club, St. Paul

Designed 1962, not built. Rendering for "suggested new design."

NOTES

Foreword

1. Thomas R. Kimball completed his MIT architectural studies in 1889 and remained in Boston to study art for a year before moving to Omaha. He was elected to the AIA College of Fellows in 1910 and served as national president from 1918 to 1920. Henry F. Whithey, *Biographical Dictionary of American Architects* (Los Angeles: Hennessey & Ingalls, 1970), p. 344–45.

2. *Journal of the Twenty-third Quadrennial Session of the General Conference of the African Methodist Episcopal Church* (Nashville: AME Sunday School Union, 1908), p. 213.

Chapter 1. To Be Young, Gifted, and Black

Chapter title from playwright Lorraine Hansberry's posthumously published book of the same name; in 1969 Nina Simone used the title for a song written in tribute to Hansberry, her long-time friend.

1. David Vassar Taylor, "Pilgrim's Progress: Black St. Paul and the Making of an Urban Ghetto 1870–1930" (Ph.D. dissertation, University of Minnesota, 1977), pp. 223–25; *Fourteenth Census of the United States 1920: Abstract of Minnesota* (Washington, D.C.: Government Printing Office, 1924); *United States Bureau of the Census: Negro Population in the United States 1790–1915* (New York: Arno Press, 1968), p. 99; Abram Harris, *The Negro Population in Minneapolis* (Minneapolis: Minneapolis Urban League and Phyllis Wheatley House, 1926), p. 11.

2. "The Man of the Month: Clarence Wesley Wigington," *Eyes* Magazine, vol. 1, no. 2 (May 1946), p. 4; *The Appeal*, March 13, 1915; July 3, 1915. *The Appeal* noted Wigington's presence in the city only months after his arrival. Between 1915 and 1920 he and his family would be mentioned regularly in the columns of that newspaper.

3. "Civil Service Bureau Notice of Examination, May 25, 1915," St. Paul Collection, St. Paul Public Library; *The Appeal*, Sept. 18, 1915; Wigington to Arthur Remington, May 15, 1964, Wigington-Pemberton Family Papers, Northwest Architectural Archives, University of Minnesota Libraries (all correspondence cited is in this collection); Richard K. Dozier, "Black Architects and the National Technical Association," *Journal of the NTA*, vol. 71, no. 3 (Fall 1997), p. 21.

4. "Form for Senior Classification: Experience and Record in Professional Practice," National Council of Architectural Registration Board, Los Angeles, Feb. 23, 1950, Wigington-Pemberton Family Papers; Wigington to Remington, April 5, 1965; Remington to Wigington, April 8, 1965; *The Appeal*, Jan. 19, 1918; *Fourteenth Census of the United States 1920; Omaha City Directory*, 1885–1908. Wesley Wigington's father, an Englishman, married a woman of mixed ancestry. Jennie Roberts was born in Fulton, Missouri, in 1853; she may have taught school in Kirkwood or Webster Grove, Missouri, before marrying Wesley Wigington.

5. *Omaha City Directory*, 1885–1908; *The Appeal*, Jan. 19, 1918. Wesley may have died in 1900; that is the last year he was listed in the city directory. Jennie died in Sheridan, Wyoming, in 1918 at age 65.

6. Wigington to Remington, May 15, 1964; "Form for Senior Classification," Feb. 23, 1950. Alfred Juergens (1866–?) contributed regularly to annual exhibitions at the Art Institute of Chicago between 1899 and 1929. His Studio-Atelier in Omaha may have been short-lived; neither he nor the studio appear in city directories. Mantle Fielding, *Dictionary of American Painters, Sculptors and Engravers* (Poughkeepsie, N.Y.: Apollo Books, 1986), p. 468. J. Laurie Wallace (1864–1953) studied at the Academy of Fine Arts in Philadelphia under Thomas Eakins. After stints as director of the Art League of Chicago, president of the Chicago Society of Art, and instructor at the Art Institute of Chicago, he was enticed to move to Omaha in 1891 by George W. Lininger, a wealthy businessman and art collector who converted his carriage house into a teaching studio for the professor. Wallace eventually became the first head of the Western Art Association and director of its school in Omaha. *Omaha World Herald*, Oct. 2, 1929; June 30, 1953.

7. Wigington to Remington, May 15, 1964; Remington to Wigington, April 8, 1965; "Form for Senior Classification," July 31, 1950. Wigington claims to have risen from junior draftsman to designer for Kimball in three years. There is some reason to doubt this account because the position of designer would have included supervisory responsibilities, which a draftsman with no prior academic training is unlikely to have assumed in a major firm.

8. Affidavit and Marriage License, State of Nebraska, Douglas County No. 21256, Clarence Wigington and Viola L. Williams, July 8, 1908, Wigington Papers.

9. *A Comprehensive Program for Historic Preservation in Omaha* (Omaha: Landmarks Heritage Preservation Commission, 1983), p. 71; *Patterns on the Landscape: Heritage Conservation in North Omaha* (Omaha: Landmarks Heritage Preservation Commission, 1984), p. 40; *The Appeal,* Jan. 19, 1918; Federal Writers Program of the WPA, *The Negroes of Nebraska* (Lincoln: Woodruff Printing Company, 1940), p. 38. The Bailey House is located at 2816 Pratt Street. The addition to St. John's A.M.E. Church was built in 1910–11; the church was destroyed by fire in 1918.

10. "Form for Senior Classification," July 31, 1950; "Form for Senior Classification," Feb. 23, 1950; *Circuit's Smart Woman,* "Clarence W. Wigington: Architect Extraordinary," Jan. 1948.

11. "Form for Senior Classification," Feb. 23, 1950; Remington to Wigington, April 8, 1965; *Eyes* Magazine; Gayle Pemberton, *Hottest Water in Chicago: Notes of a Native Daughter* (New York: Anchor Books, 1992), p. 83. Another black architect, William Sidney Pittman, is credited with designing five other buildings for the National Religious Training School in 1910. Pittman was married to Portia Washington, the daughter of Booker T. Washington.

12. *Omaha City Directory,* 1910–14. Possibly a third child, a male, was born shortly before or after their arrival in St. Paul in 1914. *The Appeal* on two occasions—July 3, 1915, and Sept. 18, 1915—made reference to three children. No birth or death certificates for this child have been located in Minnesota. In *Hottest Water in Chicago,* Pemberton states that Viola miscarried a male baby while living in Sheridan, Wyoming.

13. Projects include the Britt House (1912), 2519 Maple Street; the Thomas P. Peterson House (1912), 3908 N. Eighteenth Street, built for a white car operator for the Omaha and Council Bluffs Railway Company; the G. Wade Obee House (1913), 2518 Lake Street, built for a black undertaker; the Hollis M. Johnson House (1914), 1820 Lothrop, built for the president of the Omaha Sanitary Supply Company; the Broomfield and Crutchfield duplexes (1913), 2502–04 and 2508–10 Lake Street (the latter has been razed); an apartment building (1914), 1232–34 S. Eleventh Street; and a duplex (1914), 125–27 S. Thirty-eighth Street. On the Zion Baptist Church, located at 2215 Grant Street, see *Patterns on the Landscape* and *The Negroes of Nebraska.*

Chapter 2. Among Equals

1. W. B. Hennessy, *Past and Present of St. Paul* (Chicago: S. J. Clarke, 1906), p. 200.

2. Ernest S. Bradford, "History and Underlying Principles of Commission Government," *Commission Government in American Cities,* Annals, vol. 38, no. 3

(Nov. 1911), pp. 3–11. For St. Paul's adoption of the commission plan, see "See Merit in the Commission Plan," *St. Paul Pioneer Press*, Oct. 15, 1911; Henry A. Castle, *History of St. Paul and Vicinity* (Chicago: Lewis Publishing Co., 1912), p. 183; Charter of the City of St. Paul, 1913; *St. Paul City Directory* (R. L. Polk), 1914, pp. 17–19.

3. When local politics forced Hausler out of the City Architect's Office in 1922, he took a leave from the architectural profession to serve consecutive terms as state senator. Henry A. Castle, *Minnesota, Its Story and Biography* (Chicago: Lewis Publishing Co., 1915), pp. 1083–84; clippings file on Senator Charles A. Hausler, St. Paul Public Library.

4. Clippings file, St. Paul Public Library; "Confirm Report of Attack on Hausler," *St. Paul Pioneer Press*, Aug. 25, 1914; Personnel Archives, City of St. Paul. I am indebted to Angie Jaskinski for discovering this and other information cited below from the Personnel Archives. Hausler's appointment of Wirth was within his authority; even after the Civil Service Bureau was installed, the City Architect could make temporary appointments between exams.

5. *Annual Report*, City of St. Paul Bureau of Civil Service, 1914. An office fire and numerous bureaucratic tangles delayed completion of the construction documents of the libraries until Wigington had come into the City Architect's Office, fueling recent speculation that he had a hand in the designs. But the plans were made in the winter of 1914–15 and declared complete in April 1915, one month before Wigington sat for the Civil Service exam. *Improvement Bulletin*, Jan. 16, 1915; April 10, 1915; June 19, 1915; Nov. 20, 1915; Jan. 29, 1916.

6. *Annual Report*, City of St. Paul Bureau of Civil Service, 1915; *The Appeal*, Sept. 9, 1915. In his later years, this moment took on heroic proportions in Wigington's recollections, as the pool of exam-takers rose from 8 to 45 and the gap between his score and those of his competitors became "quite a margin." Wigington to Arthur Remington, May 15, 1964, Wigington-Pemperton Family Papers, Northwest Architectural Archives, University of Minnesota Libraries (all correspondence cited is in this collection).

7. Ricard K. Dozier, "Black Architects and the National Technical Association," *Journal of the NTA*, vol. 71, no. 3 (Fall 1997), p. 21. According to Dozier, the 1910 census counted 59 African American architects out of 10,504; in 1920 there were 50 out of 22,000; 63 in 1930; and 80 in 1940. "Sample Questions and General Information with Relation to Civil Service Examinations," vol. 1 (Sept. 1915), Civil Service Bureau of the City of St. Paul, St. Paul Collection, St. Paul Public Library.

8. "Civil Service Bureau Notice of Examination, May 25, 1915," St. Paul Collection; Personnel Archives; "Sterling Club Honors Wigington," *St. Paul Recorder*,

April 1941. Eisenmenger had been a draftsman for Thomas Holyoke and Great Northern Railway, among others.

9. Harsh criticism of the force account method occurred immediately and repeatedly in the trade press for builders; see, for example, *Improvement Bulletin*, May 22, 1915. Its ultimate downfall was due to massive cost overruns (60 percent above the estimate) on two park buildings completed in 1929. "Seeger Says Rush on Park Shelters Was Costly Error," *St. Paul Pioneer Press*, May 14, 1936.

10. *Improvement Bulletin*, Jan. 30, 1915; April 24, 1915; June 26, 1915; July 24, 1915. Ultimately, only two other schools, Como Park and Lafayette, would use the Randolph Heights floor plan. Lafayette School construction was delayed until 1923, after Hausler had been forced from his job.

11. The fact that Como Park and Homecroft elementary schools are the only projects of Hausler's tenure for which Wigington publicly claimed credit is of some significance. Were he involved in any vital way with the designs of the Carnegie branch libraries or the model school at Randolph Heights, which are commonly attributed to him, he surely would have listed them on his résumé or in his interviews for publication.

12. *The Appeal*, June 19, 1917.

13. "Form for Senior Classification: Experience and Record in Professional Practice," National Council of Architectural Registration Board, Los Angeles, July 31, 1950, Wigington-Pemberton Family Papers. It is unclear whether all of these houses were designed in 1917 or some were the result of private commissions taken on after his return to the City Architect's Office.

14. *The Appeal*, March 16, 1918.

15. Design of the Phalen Park Bathhouse and Golf Course Clubhouse, both elaborate buildings for their day, began in 1917, though the clubhouse was not constructed until 1919. Drawings in Real Estate Office Archives, City of St. Paul; *Improvement Bulletin*, Dec. 7, 1918; *Report of Department of Parks, Playgrounds, and Public Buildings of the City of St. Paul, 1914–1919*, p. 29.

16. The only architectural exam at either junior or senior level between 1915 and late 1921 was one for junior draftsmen in 1919. Prior to this exam, Godette had worked in the offices of W. D. McLeith and W. F. Keefe, both of St. Paul. Because he was assigned major drafting responsibilities in the mid-1920s, it is likely he stood for and passed the senior architectural draftsman's exam in December 1921 or July 1922. The latter was given to fill Wigington's temporarily vacated post. *Annual Report*, City of St. Paul Bureau of Civil Service, 1921 and 1922.

17. *The Appeal*, Oct. 5, 1918. A permit search has failed to turn up any Rondo Avenue bungalows built to Wigington's plans. The attribution of the two creameries was first published in "The Man of the Month, p. 5. For descriptions and pictures of the buildings, see *Twin City Milk Producers' Bulletin*, Nov. 1921, Nov. 1922, and Dec. 1925. In later years Wigington claimed to have designed four creameries. The two not mentioned in the *Eyes* article were probably the creameries at Cedar and Robbinsdale, which were expanded and remodeled rather than being built from the ground up.

18. *St. Paul Pioneer Press*, June 19, 1922; Personnel Archives. Eisenmenger was appointed earlier but left to join the armed services, returning to the office in 1919–20.

19. *Northwestern Bulletin*, Aug. 19, 1922. Another black newspaper later gave a simpler version of his resignation: the opportunity to design St. James A.M.E. Church. *St. Paul Echo*, Jan. 16, 1926. The proposals for the Pyramid Building in north Minneapolis and Gopher Lodge No. 105, Improved Benevolent Protective Order of Elks of the World, are described and illustrated in the *Minneapolis Messenger*, June 9, 1923, and the *Northwestern Bulletin-Appeal*, Jan. 17, 1925, respectively.

20. National Register of Historic Places Nomination Form, Highland Park Tower, June 1984, State Historic Preservation Office files.

21. Attribution of the Highland Park Pavilion to Wigington has been commonplace over the last decade. Both the elaborate Italian Renaissance ornamentation of the building and the lightness of its arcades are, however, foreign to Wigington's other work. The same can be said of the less-known but equally sparkling design for Newell Park. The two buildings were cited years later as preeminent examples of the force account method gone mad; Highland Park Pavilion, for example, was bid at $12,000 and estimated by the city to cost $9,000, whereas its real cost ran to $43,000. "Seeger Says Rush on Park Shelters Was Costly Error."

22. "The Man of the Month," p. 5; drawings in Real Estate Office Archives.

23. The 1930–31 transfers shuttled him back and forth between senior architectural draftsman and assistant architectural engineer; in 1944 he was briefly transferred to Public Works as an engineer. Personnel Archives.

24. For Minnesota projects funded by the Public Works Administration (PWA), see Robert A. Radford, "Activities of the Public Works Administration in Minnesota," *Northwest Architect*, vol. 1 (Nov. 1936), pp. 10–12, and "Final Report of the Minnesota Work Projects Administration: S. L. Stolte, Administrator," February 1943, copy in Sidney L. Stolte, Minnesota Works Progress Administration Records, Minnesota Historical Society. The largest PWA projects in the state were the Holman Airfield improvements and the $2 million sewage treatment facility at

Pig's Eye Lake, a swampy widening of the Mississippi River south of downtown St. Paul. Apart from these, the lion's share of PWA money in St. Paul went to recreational buildings and structures, including many of Wigington's designs for school gymnasiums, park buildings, and ski slides. The ice palaces, built by stone masons in their off-season, also qualified for PWA funding.

25. National Register of Historic Places Registration Form, Holman Field Administration Building, June 28, 1991, State Historic Preservation Office files; Paul D. Hagstrum, "City Boasts 'New' Airport," [St. Paul] *Athletic Club Events*, July 1940, p. 5.

26. Robert Olsen, "Architect to the Kings of the Carnivals: 'Cap' Wigington and His Ice Palace 'Babies'," *Ramsey County History* Magazine, Spring 2000. After a hiatus for World War II, the ice palace tradition was revived yet again in 1947, with Wigington once more submitting the winning design. Construction of it, too, was halted by warm weather.

27. Personnel Archives.

28. "City Architect Wigington to be Honored," *St. Paul Pioneer Press*, Dec. 13, 1948. The list of buildings consisted of Highland Park Water Tower, numerous ice palaces, Washington, Wilson, and Marshall high schools, an addition to Monroe High School, and Horace Mann, Edgcumbe, and Como Park elementary schools. There were minor errors in the newspaper listing: Wigington was architect of the original Monroe High School building as well as the addition, and only the Mann School addition was his.

29. "Form for Senior Classification," July 31, 1950; Wigington to Frank I. Tobin & Son, Builders, Aug. 29, 1948; Wigington to T. D. McAnulty and John A. McAnulty, Aug. 29, 1948.

30. "City Architect Wigington to be Honored"; "Form for Senior Classification," July 31, 1950; Wigington to Commissioner of Taxation, March 13, 1950.

31. Wigington to Donald F. White, Oct. 2, 1949; Minnesota State Board of Registration Certificate of Registration, Feb. 24, 1937, Wigington Papers.

32. Wigington to Walter L. McDonald, Secretary, Fidelity Lodge No. 10, Oct. 12, 1950; Wigington to George G. Smith, Aug. 22, 1955; Wigington to South Los Angeles Mortuary, Inc., March 16, 1957; Wigington to George Barker, April 11, 1965. Wigington's claim was slightly exaggerated; at least one of his lodge commissions was for supervision only and all of the identified church projects were remodelings.

33. Wigington to Margaret Harper, Nov. 20, 1958; Wigington to Bank of America, April 30, 1960; Wigington to Mutual of Omaha, Jan. 29, 1966. The year following the Wigingtons' return to St. Paul, Clarence vacated his Hamm Building office and resumed his old office address at his brother's home on Aurora Avenue.

34. Wigington to Paul Wigington, March 5, 1965; Wigington to Minnesota Highway Department, March 8, 1966; Wigington to Mutual of Omaha, Jan. 29, 1966. Viola Wigington died in 1980.

Chapter 3. A Stronger Soul within a Finer Frame

Chapter title from Claude McKay, "Baptism," Harlem Shadows (1922)

1. David Vassar Taylor, "Pilgrim's Progress: Black St. Paul and the Making of an Urban Ghetto 1870–1930" (Ph.D. dissertation, University of Minnesota, 1977), pp. 110–16.

2. Taylor, "Pilgrim's Progress," pp. 99–110.

3. *The Appeal*, July 3, 1915; June 9, 1917; Jan. 19, 1918; April 3, 1918. Frederick L. McGhee, the criminal lawyer and civil rights activist who was instrumental in founding the St. Paul chapter of the NAACP, had died a year before Wigington's arrival. History has not recorded the first meeting between Wigington and Adams.

4. Virginia Brainard Kunz, *Muskets to Missiles: A Military History of Minnesota* (St. Paul: Minnesota Statehood Centennial Commission, 1958), pp. 153–54; Circular Letter No. 3 from Adjutant General to Commanding Officer, Minnesota Home Guard, May 15, 1918, Wigington-Pemberton Family Papers, Northwest Architectural Archives, University of Minnesota Libraries (all correspondence cited is in this collection).

5. *Twin City Star*, Dec. 7, 1918.

6. *Twin City Star*, April 20, 1918; Dr. V. D. Turner to Adjutant General Rhinow, April 18, 1918; A. G. of Minnesota to Major George Earl, April 29, 1918.

7. *Twin City Star*, April 20, June 1, 1918. An article on the editorial page of the *Twin City Star*, April 13, 1918, while appreciative of the effort to establish a military organization for "cullud peepel," questioned the timing around the election. Others commissioned as captains in the 16th Battalion were Jose H. Sherwood of Company B, Gale P. Hilyer of Company C, and Charles Sumner Smith of Company D.

8. The Minnesota National Guard continued to deny access to African Americans until November 22, 1949, when an executive order signed by Governor Luther Youngdahl ended the prohibition. Clifford Edward Rucker, "The Governor's Interracial Commission of Minnesota: An Administrative History" (master's thesis, University of Minnesota, 1955), p. 39.

9. *Northwestern Bulletin*, March 25, 1922, p. 3; *St. Paul City Directory*, 1923; Mildred and Michael Bohanon, interview with Herbert Crowell, Detroit, Mich., June 6, 1998, transcript, Wigington Papers. Between 1915 and 1923, the Wigingtons lived

in six locations, all in St. Paul: 355 Arundel Street, 582 Rondo Avenue, 1020 Rondo Avenue, 495 Carroll Avenue, 603 St. Anthony Avenue, and 679 St. Anthony Avenue.

10. David Vassar Taylor, "The Blacks," *They Chose Minnesota: A Survey of the State's Ethnic Groups* (St. Paul: Minnesota Historical Society Press, 1981), p. 81. The St. Anthony Avenue neighborhood, predominantly white in the 1920s, would gradually become black during the twenty-five years the Wigingtons owned the property.

11. Muriel and Gayle Pemberton, interview with Herbert Crowell, Chicago, Ill., June 14, 1998; Bohanon interview; Gayle Pemberton, *Hottest Water in Chicago: Notes of a Native Daughter* (New York: Anchor Books, 1992), p. 90.

12. Pemberton, *Hottest Water*, p. 53; Bohanon interview.

13. *Northwestern Bulletin-Appeal*, Dec. 1, 1923, Jan. 17, 1925, June 20, 1925; James S. Griffin, interview with author, St. Paul, Feb. 13, 2000; Abram H. Weaver, "The Sterling Club, Inc., 1919–1994: A Historical Review" (typescript, n.d.), Minnesota Historical Society; Wigington to John Patton, June 30, 1958. Located on Dale Street between Carroll and Rondo avenues, the Sterling Club building was demolished for construction of Interstate 94 in the 1960s.

14. Pemberton, *Hottest Water*, pp. 37, 44. It is interesting to note that the period of Viola's absence was one of the most productive periods in Wigington's professional career, coinciding with a great deal of work for the WPA and with his service as executive secretary for the Urban League (see ensuing paragraphs). It is equally interesting to note that after Viola's return, he designed his most playful creations, the ice palaces.

15. T.S.T.C. Club Papers, Minnesota Historical Society.

16. Charles H. Wesley, *History of Sigma Pi Phi: First of Negro American Greek Letter Fraternities, 50th Anniversary Edition 1904–1954* (Washington, D.C.: Society for the Study of Negro Life and History, Inc., 1954), pp. 154–55. Charter members of the Omicron Boule were attorneys William T. Francis, William R. Morris, Raymond W. Cannon, and Miles O. Cannon; Doctors Val Do Turner and James H. Redd; the Reverend Stephen L. Theobald; and L. Raymond Hill, Elmer Morris, and Gayle P. Hilyer.

17. There was a fledgling chapter of Garvey's U.N.I.A. in the Twin Cities. *The Minneapolis Messenger*, Sept. 10, 1921; Sept. 24, 1921; Oct. 15, 1921; Nov. 19, 1921.

18. Wigington was undoubtedly also familiar with the work of Asa Phillip Randolph, leader of the Brotherhood of Pullman Porters. Randolph had visited St. Paul several times in the 1930s at the request of black Pullman railway employees attempting to unionize. Wigington counted among his friends and acquaintances numerous redcaps, porters, and waiters employed by the railway companies,

and the abuse and indignities regularly suffered by them were well documented and well known throughout the black community. Though sympathetic to their cause, Wigington did not appear to be active in that struggle.

19. Board members guide, 1959, roll 2, microfilm M251, St. Paul Urban League Records, Minnesota Historical Society.

20. Taylor, "The Blacks," p. 82; Taylor, "Pilgrim's Progress," pp. 224–25. St. James A.M.E. Church used its newsletter, the "Helper," to post employment and housing opportunities. Copies of the "Helper" are in the Eva Neal and Family Papers, Minnesota Historical Society.

21. Whitney M. Young, Jr., "History of the St. Paul Urban League" (Plan B paper, University of Minnesota, 1947, copy in Minnesota Historical Society), pp. 15–21; Taylor, "The Blacks."

22. Young, "History of the St. Paul Urban League," pp. 22–25, 28. The Urban League, like the NAACP, often chose white business, political, or religious leaders to chair its interracial boards.

23. *You May Quote Us on This!*, p. 6, copy in Minnesota Historical Society.

24. Wigington to the Honorable Edward J. Thye, Governor, Sept. 5, 1944; Griffin interview. Wigington used his position as president of the Twin Cities Service Men's Council to petition Governor Thye to intercede in hiring Sidney Salter, a World War I veteran who had encountered discrimination in his pursuit of employment as a fireman-engineer.

25. James S. Griffin, "Blacks in the St. Paul Police Department: An Eighty-Year Survey," *Minnesota History*, vol. 44, no. 7 (Fall 1975), pp. 258–60.

26. Griffin, "Blacks in the St. Paul Police Department," pp. 260–65.

27. *Twin Cities Herald*, April 9, 1932; *Minneapolis Spokesman*, Dec. 27, 1939; Governor Luther W. Youngdahl to Wigington, July 27, 1948.

28. Rucker, "The Governor's Interracial Commission," pp. 1–8. The St. Paul Urban League also conducted a survey on behalf of the commission, sent out to 2,231 employers and 452 labor unions, to discern attitudes that might be detrimental to the employment of Negroes. Although only 600 surveys were returned, the results were published in a pamphlet titled "The Negro Worker" (May 10, 1945).

29. Pemberton, *Hottest Water,* p. 70.

30. Richard K. Dozier, "Black Architects and the National Technical Association," *Journal of the NTA*, vol. 71, no. 3 (Fall 1997), p. 19.

31. Wigington to Donald F. White, Oct. 2, 1949, March 19, 1950, Oct. 17, 1950.

32. Wigington to White, Oct. 17, 1950; Wigington to Calvin L. McKissack, Oct. 17, 1950; Wigington to James C. Evans, Nov. 9, 1950.

Chapter 4. Architectural Legacy

1. "The Man of the Month: Clarence Wesley Wigington," *Eyes* Magazine, vol. 1, no. 2 (May 1946), p. 5; National Register of Historic Places Nomination Form, Highland Park Tower, June 1984, State Historic Preservation Office files.

2. Wigington's initials on the plans for a 1939 addition to Horace Mann Elementary School have misled some into attributing the original building design to him. His addition follows Buetow's design, especially its ornamentation, very closely.

3. "Conventions—A Major Industry," *St. Paul Magazine,* Summer 1931, pp. 19–20.

4. "Dedication to be Sunday," *St. Paul Pioneer Press,* undated article in St. Paul Parks clippings file, St. Paul Public Library. The last of the rusticated stone playground buildings, the Baker recreation building was designed in 1938 and opened in 1939.

5. "This Ark Planned for Como Park," *St. Paul Dispatch,* March 18, 1935; "Como Birds and Beasts to Return to Noah's Ark—An $80,000 One," *St. Paul Pioneer Press*, March 18, 1935. A presentation drawing of the ark is credited to City Architect Bassford by the *Dispatch* article, and the *Pioneer Press* reporter credited him with drafting the plans, though the working drawings clearly bear Wigington's initials as architect in charge. One plausible scenario would have Bassford initiating the idea with a sketch and Wigington carrying it out.

6. "Bring 'em Back Helps Lay Zoo Cornerstone," *St. Paul Dispatch,* Feb. 11, 1936; "Como Park Animals Go Ritzy; Ultra Modern Zoo Is Reason," *St. Paul Pioneer Press,* [March 1936], St. Paul Parks clippings file, St. Paul Public Library.

Chapter 5. Who Will Speak for Me

1. Gayle Pemberton, *Hottest Water in Chicago: Notes of a Native Daughter* (New York: Anchor Books, 1992), pp. 74–79.

2. It is interesting to note that black stonecutters from Georgia were imported to assist in the building of the Minnesota State Capitol at the turn of the twentieth century. White laborers were considered not skilled enough to work with marble. Several of the black stonecutters settled in the Twin Cities. *The Appeal,* May 1, 1920.

3. Pemberton, *Hottest Water,* p. 84.

INDEX